Lynn Farley-Rose

How I Learned to Stop
SALUTING MAGPIES

A Lifeline List and Letting Go of Fear

Copyright © 2025 by Lynn Farley-Rose

Lynn Farley-Rose asserts her moral right to be identified as the author of this book. All rights reserved. This book or any portion thereof may not be reproduced or used in any manner whatsoever without the express written permission of the publisher except for the use of brief quotations in a book review.

I have tried to recreate events, places and conversations from my memories of them. In order to maintain their anonymity I have changed the names of some individuals.

Paperback ISBN 978-0-9934711-2-4

Cover design by Jo Dalton
Interior design by Furkan Süperdoğan

Published in the UK and USA

Esmeralda Publishing
60treatsandmore@gmail.com

*Happiness is neither virtue nor pleasure
nor this thing nor that but simply growth.
We are happy when we are growing.*

WB Yeats

*Happiness is neither virtue nor pleasure
nor this thing nor that but simply growth.
We are happy when we are growing.*

WB Yeats

*For **Rita**,*
with love and decades of gratitude

Contents

2013 11
Introduction 13
The List 17

2014 23
Spirulina 25
Keeping my head 31
Relying on myself 35
The Jewel in the Crown 41
Conundrums 45
Unexpected benefits 51
Old ways, new ways 55
Golden tickets 59
Dancing in the dark 63
Not guilty 69
Just a jacket 75
Edging along in Berlin 81
Thorns 87
18 Folgate Street 89
Feel don't think 93
Adapting 97
A new home 103
Reader's block 107

2015 111
Simplify 113
Riding on branch lines 119
Where did you park? 123
Fifty-two films 127
The Fifth Battle of Mansfield Park 133
Awkward questions 139
Trapped 145

2016 149
Fear of painting 151
The end of a walk 157
Dutch courage 161
Ruts 167
Things change 169
Two poems 175
Honeymoons 179
Slow living 183
Provincial life 191
Finding It 197
Flamingos 203

2017 209
A better understanding 211
Reframing 219
Spring rain 225
Making my peace 229
A shock 233
A windfall 239

Pass it on 243
Savouring the Fall 249
Being here 257

2018 265
Extra time 267
Challenging the magpies 273
Standing on shoulders 281
Esmeralda's secrets 289
Experimenting with forgiveness 295

2019 301
Not the end 303
State of wonder 311
Epilogue: A new list 319

Appendices 325
The Complete List of 60 Treats 327
Fish recipes 331
Further Reading 343
Acknowledgements 351

2013

Introduction

Daffodils and primroses grow in clumps along the side of the road, brightening what is already a cheerful day, and ponies roam freely, holding up the cars as they wander along in search of the next patch of juicy grass. They're sturdy and compact, refusing to be hurried. There's no rush for me either. I'm relaxed as I drive through the New Forest with Mike next to me, long legs stretched out, and stylish sunglasses on his nose. We've got all day. This is our sixth date. Or maybe it's our seventh. I'm losing count.

I'm loving his company but I can't avoid noticing that the magpies are out in force today, hopping around at the edge of the road – some on their own and some in pairs. They're tricksy birds. When I see a singleton, I raise my hand to my head in salute. And whisper 'Good Morning, Mr Magpie. How's your wife?' I can ignore the pairs, as two magpies together symbolise joy. But like I said, they are tricksy and often when I see what appears to be a lone magpie and have my hand half-way to my head, a jaunty companion will hop out of the undergrowth so that I have to unravel the salute with a sweeping downwards movement. No-one's ever told me that you have to do this.

But it's best to be safe.

The air is still and it's warm in the car as I focus on the road in front. The chat flows easily with so much to explore in this early, wary phase. Mike was widowed three years ago in 2010 and it's just over a year since my long marriage with Shaun came to a shuddering halt. He's met my two teenage children and we're discussing plans for a weekend that might include the other two who are in their early twenties. Then I notice that he's gone quiet, and I see from the corner of my eye that he is staring at me.

'What are you doing?' he says. 'Why do you keep jerking your arm up to your head?'

'It's the old magpie rhyme,' I say, smiling. 'You know – One for sorrow, two for joy…'

I expect this to clarify things. But he looks mystified. Then I realise…

It must be because he grew up in South Africa.

So I spell it out more clearly. 'If you see a magpie on its own you have to say hello. And if you don't do it right it will get offended and give you bad luck.'

My earnest explanation doesn't seem to help and as we pass a thatched pub, he suggests that we stop for a drink. We sit in the garden under a blue and white parasol, and he quizzes me. 'You talk to magpies? Is that a family thing? Is there other stuff I need to know about?'

I take a sip of ginger beer and a deep breath, and try once more to justify the saluting. My life has been turbulent for the past few years – and I daren't risk making things worse so I have to keep the magpies sweet. As I say the words out loud for the first time ever, even I have to admit that it all sounds rather implausible.

'But you have a scientific training,' he says, 'like me.'

And I do.

Different from my mother where all this started. She had a lot of bad luck and she fended off further ambushes by refusing to allow an open umbrella indoors and never knowingly giving houseroom to a bluebell. She also told me that if you put your clothes on inside out then you must *not* correct your mistake. Perhaps she gave lip service to that – I don't recall her looking odd. On the other hand, she may have taken it so much to heart that she took extra care when getting dressed.

As I do.

The List

When I was ten my mother made two announcements that astonished me, and upended the drab claustrophobia of our life together. The first was that we were going to live with my sister and her young family in Scotland. It was only a temporary arrangement but it was still the most exciting thing that had ever happened. I'd barely been outside Devon – let alone England. And not only would I get to spend time with my big sister but I'd be going to a new school.

The second announcement was that she, my mother, was having a nervous breakdown.

I had no idea what this meant. But I *did* know that she'd been even more grumpy than usual. And she'd been crying a lot. She worked evenings in a hotel bar and she said that having a nervous breakdown made it impossible for her to do that. My father wasn't any help. He lived miles away and was always breaking the promises he made about sending envelopes of money through the post. We hardly ever saw him and I knew enough about the precarious state of our finances to realise that this nervous breakdown was a worrying development.

She explained, too, that the nervous breakdown affected her writing and that sometimes she couldn't remember how to spell. I'd noticed that and had been really surprised when she'd asked me how to spell 'and'. I would have thought she was joking if she hadn't looked so terrified. She was very upset when she told me about the writing, and as she said it quite a few times I guessed that not being able to spell must be the defining feature of a nervous breakdown. It was how you would know if you were having one.

Following her astonishing announcement there were still a couple of weeks to get through before we could set off on our train journey to Glasgow, and during that time she seemed shapeless – slopping outside the boundaries of being my mum. 'I'm in a state,' she would flap, flushed and breathing so fast that she had to keep her sentences short. I had a washed-around, sinking feeling and lost myself in reading.

Mercifully, things improved a great deal while we were in Scotland. My mother made herself useful helping my sister with her toddler and new baby, and I was welcomed into a friendly group of children. As we all skipped through the woods to the village school each morning, I knew I'd be coming home at the end of the day to a family. I was no longer on my own with my mother's fears.

At the end of that summer, we returned to Devon for the start of my final year at primary school and unexpectedly, my father moved in with us. I barely knew him as he'd gone away when I was two. My mother got a new job in a chemist's shop which meant she didn't have to work in the evening anymore, and she rarely referred to her breakdown after that. I didn't think about it much, for decades. But during recent years, the spectre of shapelessness has come back to haunt me. I'm reassured that there's nothing amiss with my spelling, but I do feel adrift.

It's been twenty-three years since Will went to playgroup, setting off on the long educational road where his siblings Emma, Henry and Molly later joined him. This means that for twenty-three years I've been walking this road too – making packed lunches, turning up for parents' evenings, finding lost sports kit, and the patchwork of other things that have kept life busy. We've all faced forward and each stage has been clearly signposted. But now the eldest two have graduated, and Henry is at university. Molly is doing her GCSEs next year, and with that milestone, I'm aware that the end of this particular road is in sight. On top of this impending change is ongoing chaos from the divorce. There are some big decisions to make about where to live and what I'm for.

These are daunting questions and although I don't yet see a clear way forward, the one thing I am certain of is that I must avoid feelings of shapelessness and being washed around.

Fortunately, I have something that might help.

Some months ago in the summer of 2011, I made a list. This was before I knew about the divorce and was in the wake of some difficult years when Shaun, my husband, had been ill with cancer, and we'd faced financial catastrophe and had to sell our beloved house. I jotted down sixty things that I was eager to do in the seven and a half years leading up to my next milestone birthday, and which were not luxuries but instead experiences that I thought would be enjoyable and enriching. They were chosen for no other reason than that I wanted to do them – and so I called them treats.

I believed I was simply coming up with a way to have some fun and re-engage with life after recent challenges, and years of raising children. But what I didn't see at the time was that it provided me with a structure that could challenge the shapelessness I'd seen in my mother. The shapelessness that I dreaded. It was important that the structure was solid. I'd spent years longing to do certain things but with the shifting sands of parenthood, it was hard to focus. Now, with the list, I had an immutable supply of activities to draw upon. 'But you can change it as you go through, can't you?' said my pragmatic friend Esther. 'No' I said firmly, the very idea making me panic. For better – or sometimes worse as it turned out, my list was fixed.

I know that many people don't like lists. In fact, some people get quite cross when I mention them. They get defensive and complain that they're limiting – that they kill spontaneity. But my list isn't at all like that. Although it is a framework, it doesn't have a rigid schedule. That would start to feel like a burden. Instead, the idea is to let each treat have its moment when there's a reason to do it. Perusing the list and deciding which to pick next is like choosing from a classy box of chocolates.

I got off to a great start with forays into travel, magic, cookery, modern art, and Shakespeare. But within six months, Shaun and I separated – and with that everything changed. Friends and family offered patient ears, warm hearts and steady shoulders but ultimately I had to find my own way through the fog. And it was at this point that the treats stepped up. Like the best of friends, they revealed hidden depths in a crisis, offering distractions and signposts. The *River Cafe Cookery Book* treat cajoled me into preparing and eating delicious Italian dishes when I'd lost interest in food, and the dread of my first separated wedding anniversary was softened by a trip to New York with Henry and Molly. Horse riding lessons were a distraction, too, providing an hour each week when I had to concentrate so hard on staying seated that I got some respite from ruminating about where it all went wrong. *31 Treats And A Marriage* tells the story of how that first batch got me through. Slightly more than half the entire list in those first two years.

That leaves twenty-nine still to explore in the next five and a half years, and I'm hoping that this batch of treats will be more about thriving than merely surviving. I'm looking forward to flamingos…falling leaves…the tick of a clock…great novels…long walks…suspense…dancing in the dark…a pointed mountain…a watery fantasyland…maybe even some family mysteries. Each of these experiences, and many others, will challenge and change me in ways I cannot yet know. They will form the basis of a new, very different kind of list. And while I'm not ready to ignore the magpies yet, maybe it *is* time to take a few risks.

2014

Spirulina

It's midday on the first Friday of the year and my solicitor has just sent an email. I let it sit in my inbox for several hours. I'll need a full cafetière of strong coffee next to me when I read it but I'm not ready yet so I go for a walk to the park, do a couple of circuits round the duckpond and work up a sweat walking back up the hill. I've been expecting this email, and although I dread reading it, I know I have to.

When I do face up to it, there are no surprises. It informs me in cold, official language that my *decree nisi* has been approved and is about to be granted. This means that by the beginning of next week, after thirty years of marriage, Shaun and I will be divorced. It's a struggle to refer to *my decree nisi*, *my decree absolute*, *my* separation, *my* divorce, as these were never things I aspired to. But this email confirms that they are now inevitable and so I need to take ownership.

On Monday morning I wake up with a headache and a sinking sensation. It's that feeling again like being at the bottom of a pit – I scrabble but keep slipping and falling back down. Mid-morning, I cry and sob violently. This is a surprise as I thought the intensity was over. It feels like it will never, ever stop so I throw some coffee together and go back to bed to listen to *Woman's Hour*, which is usually a reliable distraction. But today there's a harrowing interview with Judith Tebbutt who while on holiday in Kenya, was kidnapped by Somali pirates and kept hostage for six months. Her husband was murdered. Jane Garvey is gentle. 'How on earth did you cope?' she asks and Judith describes how she kept her thoughts about her husband and son in imaginary filing cabinet drawers so she could take them out when she wanted and close them away, too. I lift my coffee mug and stop half-way to my mouth – all those years with Shaun and now I've got no idea where to file him.

Laptop on chest, I sink into the sheets and lie sleepless but exhausted. I simply don't know what else to do. But it's terribly boring and around midday I sit bolt upright. I've had enough of this. And I've had enough of feeling awful. It's not just emotional woes – my body has been making odd complaints for months.

Determined to feel better, I start by focusing on one of my most tiresome symptoms – ferocious belching. I google it and find a comprehensive list of over two hundred potential causes. The first one that catches my eye is Asiatic porpoise poisoning. This isn't much help so I give up on that and decide that perhaps a detox is the way to go. This has proved useful in the past when I've felt physically low and this time it might also exorcise bad feelings. I'll have to cut out caffeine, wheat, dairy and sugar and also introduce a few supplements. An internet article suggests a cocktail of vitamins and minerals, as well as spirulina – a dried blue-green algae that is rich in protein. It's said to have many benefits. I don't have the energy to question it – I order everything that's recommended.

On Friday morning I start the new regime and within a few hours I have a promising but temporarily debilitating sign of progress – a caffeine withdrawal headache. Saturday is a write-off but by the time my elder daughter, Emma, comes to visit on Sunday I enjoy putting together a simple meal of prawns, salmon and a big fresh salad, followed by baked nectarines. We chat about her life in London, where she shares a flat with her schoolfriend Anna, and as always she makes me laugh. After lunch, I disappear into the kitchen to make peppermint tea and to tackle the algae for the first time. I stare at the contents of the packet, which are intensely indigo and as fine as talcum powder. I've mislaid my glasses – there's no prospect of deciphering the tiny-print instructions and so I plunge in with a teaspoon and take a mouthful. This turns out to be a big mistake. The superfine powder clags all over the roof of my mouth and trickles down my throat in sticky lumps. I gag and try to get my breath while producing squeaky, choking noises.

Emma notices that I've been gone for a while and calls out, 'Everything alright Mum?'

I welcome her loving concern but it sends me into more of a panic. Even though I may be about to expire, the primitive desire to protect my offspring remains strong. She will be traumatised if she finds me gasping with blue teeth, and green foam dribbling from my nostrils. I concentrate very hard indeed and manage a reassuring grunt.

As soon as I can breathe, I rush dry-mouthed to the bathroom where I spend five minutes gulping from the cold tap and spitting. Then I clean my teeth and return to the kitchen to finish making the tea.

The next day I'm having breakfast when I remember that it's time to take some more of the dreadful stuff. It's so expensive that I don't want to waste it, so I stir two teaspoons into my liquorice tea. It's like drinking a swamp. On Tuesday I try stirring it into soya yogurt. It reminds me of indigo-coloured poster paint. On Wednesday I try to cheer it up by adding some banana.

It's time to admit to myself that none of this is helping. I'm desperate to get on with my life but I don't know what that is. So for the next few months, uncertain what else to do, I bury myself in work – writing about careers and universities for an educational publisher – and in sorting out the house. I excavate my possessions. Burrowing deep into cupboards. Making endless trips to the tip and charity shops, and filling Sainsbury's shopping bags with books, CDs and photos that Shaun might want. This demarcation of him and me, and the demarcation of mine that I want to keep and mine that I don't, feels like a necessary part of working out who I will become.

It's now over a year into my relationship with Mike and we've got into a pattern of seeing one another most weekends. We live about a hundred miles apart as he's based in Hampshire and I'm in Kent. He is kind, intelligent, funny and steady. Our relationship is helping on the long slow path to rebuilding my trust in relationships. But it is complicated as he is still grieving for his late wife and I am raw with divorce. We were introduced by a mutual friend and in some ways it came too soon. I don't want to lose him as he is undoubtedly a good thing. But I want a break and as Winter thaws into Spring I tell him I need a couple of weekends to myself to work through tangled feelings. 'I do understand,' he says and I am grateful for his maturity.

It's time to get back to the walking.

Several years ago I made a start on the North Downs Way which stretches from commuter-belt Farnham to the big skies of

Dover. It's a treat and a National Trail – each section providing respite with time to colour in however I want. Dipping in and out of the landscape, following the wooden signposts with their acorn symbols, and relishing the ongoing mystery of never knowing what's going to unfold beyond that bend in the distance. Emma and her sister Molly walked the first few sections with me. These were chatty and companionable and we covered about sixty miles. Then Shaun left and after that, along with many other things, my walking came to a halt.

Keeping my head

It's a Sunday morning in April and I'm on my way to resume my North Downs Way walk at Wrotham where the previous section ended two years ago. The drive northwards through Kent takes about forty minutes and I sing along to the radio. But as I get close to the tennis courts where I finished last time, I silence the music and myself.

I park, put on my walking boots, salute a nearby magpie, and take a deep breath. It's a serendipitous place at which to resume as my guidebook tells me that this is the half-way point between Farnham and Dover. It also tells me that Henry VIII was in this village when he received confirmation that Anne Boleyn's execution had been carried out. I have to count my blessings – I had no option but to accept that my marriage was over but at least I've kept my head.

Leaving the village, I cross a bridge over the M20 and soon after I'm on the North Downs Way. Too late, I have an image of my walking poles, poking out of the umbrella stand at home. I could do with them as there's been a lot of rain and it's sticky underfoot. I swing my leg over a stile, my boots so clogged with mud that I have to hold on carefully to the wooden bar, and then puff uphill along the edge of a field. My limbs haven't fully woken up yet, so it's a struggle, but eventually it levels out and I sit for a while, looking back across the long ploughed fields to the basin below. I stretch out my legs and realise I am grinning to myself, cheeks aching in the wind and elated with the joy of independence.

On my way again, I spot a signpost. One of the weathered wooden fingers bears a round yellow symbol with an arrow pointing to my left. It leads me up a muddy path that becomes progressively narrower until it is little more than a ledge above a dense patch of trees. I push my way through bushes and brambles as tiny thorns snag my fingers. 'Keep going,' I say and eventually I emerge from the tangle. I'm standing next to a low brick wall surrounding a detached house with a washing line, vegetable beds and a large patch of lawn. But before I can assess the damage to my hands and pride, three huge German Shepherd dogs leap up onto the wall and bark – powerful wolf teeth gleaming, dark ears pointed, and glassy eyes locked onto me. I hear my heart pounding and expect to be savaged at any moment as I struggle to hold back the tears. 'Don't provoke. Move slowly,' I think – very quietly. It's clear that I've taken the wrong path and there's no option but to turn back, so I do this as smoothly as I can until the dogs lose interest and stop barking. Then I push my way through the brambles as quickly as possible. Back at the signpost I see that I followed the wrong wooden finger. The one without the National Trail acorn symbol. I feel foolish and pray there were no CCTV cameras to record my shame.

I set off in what seems to be the right direction and before long, I'm enjoying more sweeping views of quiet Sunday fields and clumps of trees. And a rosy glow of relief. A round man in a navy bobble hat comes along with a red setter. I greet him cheerily which surprises both of us and he grunts grudgingly.

I walk on up rutted tracks, across open fields and through damp woods. Past straggly cowslips and the haze of early bluebells. These beautiful flowers bring to mind my mother, with her superstitious fear of bringing them into the house. And as I think of my mother, I remember waking on teenage Sunday mornings to her angry voice locked with my father in a cycle of frustration.

Later in the morning came the smell of gravy, the dutiful vegetable steam, and the sounds of *Family Favourites*. There was probably nothing wrong with it but it just happened to come onto the radio on Sunday, so that made it dismal and I hated it. I carried that hatred of Sundays for a long time but as an adult I found ways of bending them into a better shape with family meals, games and walks. Now I'm wary again.

There's no breeze to stir the leaves. It's just me that's moving. On and on until midday when I perch on a tree trunk in a shady spot and unpack my flask – time for hot coffee and lemon drizzle cake. This part of the North Downs Way coincides with the medieval pilgrim's route from Winchester to Thomas Becket's shrine at Canterbury Cathedral. It's comforting to know I am walking the path of so many who have gone before, seeking help for their troubles. And it's no linguistic coincidence that the words travel and travail are similar, as early journeys were arduous, and especially those of pilgrims. Here in this ancient broadleaf wood, it would be no surprise to bump into a silent, brown-robed monk. I take out my phone for the first time and see a text from my friend Rachel. 'Enjoy your pilgrimage,' she says.

In her book *Wanderlust: A History of Walking*, Rebecca Solnit writes that walking is a bodily labour that produces nothing but thoughts, experiences and arrivals. And today I can feel the rhythm of my feet working magic on me. I step between the past, the present and the future, striding out my fears, frustrations and hopes. I've tried meditation but at the moment it doesn't help. My mind feels taut and full whereas walking dissipates the energy and releases it, thought by thought.

I treasure this time on my own. Not having to worry whether my companion wants to chat or be quiet, if they're enjoying the walk, and if they want to gaze at the view or stop for a nap under a tree…There's no room for speech in solitude and today that feels good. It's a comfortable void unlike the sharp, lonely absence of speech that comes from living alongside someone with whom there are no safe topics left. Shaun and I piled pressures on ourselves. They pushed us into difficult corners, and then we had a seasoning of bad luck that stripped the words away.

There may be no speech but this North Downs solitude is not silent. A helicopter passes overhead, and farm vehicles clatter on the slopes of a distant field. And then there are the sounds that I love to hear. The crunch of my feet on twigs, and in amongst the birdsong the occasional *zwee* of a greenfinch, so distinct but rarely seen.

Later, in the thin afternoon sunshine I walk along a quiet lane, past a couple of stone cottages. One has a well-tended patch of garden at the front, with wallflowers in dusty shades of orange and yellow. They remind me of my father. Of his quiet enjoyment of gardening, and how he would retreat to digging and pruning to escape my mother's nagging.

By the time I reach Cuxton I've covered ten miles, and in that space I've been elated, strong, scared, sad, numb, raw, angry, composed, exhausted, pessimistic, hopeful and hungry. I'm glad to have walked this alone.

Relying on myself

All week I feed off the memory of my solitary walk and now that I've overcome my block on restarting, I'm keen to do another section as soon as I can. Molly is with her father this weekend so I have plenty of free time. Saturday doesn't work out as it's uncompromisingly wet but Sunday morning brings the promise of intermittent sunshine and I set off for Cuxton. The drive is just under an hour, and at ten o'clock *The Archers* actors crowd into the car, keeping me company, their voices familiar and steady.

Last weekend's walk boosted my confidence but even so it's a struggle to ignore misgivings about walking alone through remote parts of the countryside. My mother may have died many years ago, but she's still with me, whispering in my ear, 'Do be careful, dear. Do take care. Don't walk under any ladders.' I'm happy with my own company but only when things go as planned. It won't need much to go wrong for the day to be a disaster. What if I slip and twist my ankle? What if there's no phone signal? I might be stranded for days and get eaten by wild boar. What if I get struck by lightning? What if…what if…

What if…

The one thing I know for certain is that today's cake is banana bread, made yesterday from a bunch of overripe fruit.

It's studded with sultanas soaked in brandy and I'm looking forward to it.

It always takes a while to loosen up and this morning's start is easy, along tree-lined lanes and through gently sloping fields. I'm lulled into bucolic meditation but it's not long before twenty-first century infrastructure intrudes. The Medway Bridge is three bridges – two carriageways of the M2 motorway and a railway viaduct. I see a plaque on the newest of the motorway bridges and read that in 2003 the Concrete Society gave it a special award citing outstanding merit in the use of concrete. And not wanting to be left out, the railway viaduct has a plaque commemorating what *it* did in 2003. A Eurostar train sped across it at 208mph setting a UK rail speed record.

Another sign reminds anyone feeling desperate that the Samaritans are always available to help and I recall a couple of times just after the separation, when I rang for support in the middle of the night. 'I'm not suicidal,' I said sitting on the concrete garage floor, so as not to be overheard by any wakeful offspring. 'But I'm so scared, and sad and angry that I don't know what to do with it all.'

Yet another sign points to Borstal – the village where the first youth detention centre was built, in 1902. The term *Borstal* has now been replaced by *youth custody centre* but the link with this area has spread as far as India which still has a number of youth detention centres called Borstal schools.

On the far side, I walk up a long field and at the entrance to a small wood come across a microwave, discarded hiking boots, a headless doll, and a stained mattress. This is all next to a council sign reminding would-be fly-tippers that it is 'Unsightly, Irresponsible, Antisocial, and Illegal.' The noise of the motorway is difficult to ignore but I'm peckish so I perch on a damp log and attempt to shut out the ugly side of human life as I refuel with banana bread and coffee. I switch on my phone and there's a gentle ping. It's a message from Mike wishing me a happy day. We're still on a break – I don't want to find I've drifted into a new relationship because I can't cope on my own.

As I set off again it starts to rain heavily so I take my red cagoule out of my rucksack and slip it on. It may be thin but it keeps the water out. It was with me for the earlier sections of the North Downs Way – the ones I did with Molly and Emma – and now it's a talisman. A comforting connection to family. I've had it for years – and I've no idea where it came from. It was probably left by a ditzy teenager back in the days when the house was full of the children's friends. It's scruffy with mysterious black stains on the sleeves. Bicycle oil maybe.

Across another field, and then some woodland provides respite from the driving rain as I plod on with my head down and my wet fringe clinging to my forehead. The trees are still and I imagine animals taking shelter, peeping out and waiting for the downpour to stop. I'm dreamy and relaxed.

Then in an instant everything changes.

I feel a firm tap on my shoulder. So firm that it can only be deliberate. There is someone here in this deserted place and they want something from me. My heart leaps into action and I whip round, peering out from under my hood, rain running down my face. I force myself to look left and right. 'I know you're there,' I shout, surprised by the strength of my voice. 'What do you want?'

No response. There's no-one to be seen. But my mind's eye is working at top speed and conjures up plenty to see. There's a shadowy figure lurking behind the trees. Now there are several of them and they shamble towards me, radiating power and malice. One has an axe. My mother was right. The world *is* scary. Whatever was I thinking of, coming here on my own? Testing myself like this.

I shout again. My voice is shaky now and still there's no response. Just drip...drip...drip...

I walk as fast as I can towards the far edge of the trees, doing my best to look normal in case *they're* nearby. Watching me. And enjoying my fear. My heart is still pounding and I stumble, thinking that I hear footsteps rustling through the wet leaves. I keep going, desperate to get out of the woods into the open fields where there are fewer places for *them* to hide. But when no-one appears, my breathing slows down and as the panic subsides, I scan back over the evidence. The only rational conclusion is that I've just been terrified by a large splash of water falling on my shoulder. I feel idiotic and small. And then as the rain stops and the sky opens out above, my strides lengthen and I give an involuntary sigh of relief. I'm proud that I coped and that I proved my mother wrong.

All is well. The trees, hedges and fields are soothing, predictable and quietly supportive in a way that city streets never can be with their urban jolts. Then I have an uncomfortable thought – I've got no cash. With a teenager in the house, I never manage to keep any money in my purse for long and I was so engrossed with *The Archers* this morning that I forgot to top-up at an ATM. My endpoint today is a small village and my convoluted journey back to the car involves three different buses – we're still in the era before tap-on tap-off, and they only take cash. For now, though, there's nothing I can do but try to put the problem out of my mind and enjoy the walk.

A couple of miles later, I come to a junction where the path crosses a main road and I spot a Shell garage a short distance away – there's sure to be some cash there. I look at the front, the sides, through the windows, and at the back where the bins are. But there is no ATM. So I go into the shop and choose a few useful items – a packet of tissues, some biscuits and a birthday card.

'If I pay by card, would you give me some cash?' I ask as politely as I can.

'No,' replies the cashier and I feel foolish so I buy the items anyway.

'Where are you going?' she asks, looking at my muddy boots, and when I tell her that I'm heading for Detling, she laughs ominously. 'That's a long way,' she says. Another customer joins in – a woman with sensible brown shoes, a short grey perm and a small, tired-looking dog on a lead. She nods and narrows her eyes.

This is unsettling and I'm not sure how to solve the cash problem. All I can do is to keep on walking and hope for the best. Like my mother, I've spent much of my life worrying about things that didn't happen. And perversely while these things were distracting me, a whole lot of other things that I'd never considered, gnawed at my ankles and brought me down with a crash. I worried about my health, and about the children's health and happiness. But I never thought that Shaun and I would run out of money. I never thought that we would have to sell our home. I never thought that he, who gave such careful attention to diet and exercise, would get cancer in his forties. And I never *ever* thought that we would divorce.

Eventually I reach the end of my walk in the small village of Detling and spot a man coming out of his cottage. He has the habitual stoop of a tall man who struggles with low ceilings. 'Is there a cash point in the village?' I ask.

He laughs. It's clearly a ridiculous idea. I must look damp and crestfallen though, so he softens. 'The pub takes cards,' he says. 'They'll probably give you some cash if you buy a drink.'

A few minutes later, I'm sipping a lemonade at the Cock Horse with four five-pound notes in my pocket. I could have called a taxi and asked the driver to stop at an ATM but it's a personal challenge to use public transport on these walks and I'm so blinkered by this that it didn't occur to me until later. It takes over two hours to get back to Cuxton on my three Sunday-afternoon buses but I don't care at all. I'm happy to have solved a problem.

Molly is at home when I get back and tells me that she had a good weekend. I'm glad to tell her that I did too.

The Jewel in the Crown

My head is a jumble of conflicting scenarios. On the one hand, I slide back to the past and wonder whether Shaun and I could have made a go of things. Might we have clawed our way back and recreated a stable family life? Would we have had enough shared interests that we could be happy together, post-children? Could we have tried harder?

Because we both liked what we had, once. I know we did. Every day I find myself getting caught up in these speculations but there's nowhere to go with them and they take up a lot of energy. I need to find a way to rein them in as the ones that deserve my attention are the ones that keep me facing forwards.

Is this how my mother felt? Tired and confused. It makes it hard to tackle even the simplest of day-to-day decisions.

One tactic is a short to-do list. Three is a good number – not intimidating but still a framework. *Get dressed* and *clean teeth* appear quite often and working through them one by one, in order, helps to fend off the sinking feeling that goes with being overwhelmed. Sometimes one of these lists is all that's needed to put me on track for the whole day. Other times I muddle through with a life-raft of lists. The best are those that include something to look forward to at the end of the day – a reward for trudging through mundane tasks.

The three-item lists continue to punctuate many days and so it is that one evening after dinner I find myself with a piece of scrap paper that reads –

Feed cats
Sew button on Molly's school skirt
Watch Episode One of The Jewel in the Crown

The first and second were crossed off earlier. The third is a reward at the end of a working day and has been plucked from my treats list. It's a television milestone that I missed in 1984 and I've been curious about it ever since. Set against the tense backdrop of the Indian independence movement it depicts the closing years of British rule in India and is based on Paul Scott's *Raj Quartet* which begins with *The Jewel in the Crown*. At the time it was hailed as 'important television with a deep insight into India,' and its character development and stunning settings were praised. In 2010, The Guardian's Alexandra Coghlan said that it sits alongside *Brideshead Revisited* as the high-water mark of 1980s British TV.

I close the curtains, switch on the lamps, and get the fire started. Then I make a pot of coffee, break off a few squares of Lindt chocolate and grab a soft blanket.

It opens with magisterial music and jerky news footage of George V and Queen Mary's imperial visit to India in 1911. There are elephants, ermine, and hundreds of Indian soldiers. They look as though they're ready for anything but without being sure what that might be. By the end of the first episode, I'm immersed in the story.

Over the next few weeks, I watch the entire fourteen hours. There are many layers. Indian characters rage against centuries of exploitation and oppression, and there's sickening racism. Even amongst themselves, the British show appalling snobbery. One officer sneers about a colleague, 'I say, what awful chaps you come across nowadays. That fellow over there – the sort you meet in pubs on the Kingston Bypass.' Another sniffs disdainfully about one of his colleagues being a grammar school boy.

As often happens, a treat sparks curiosity and I like to be thorough so I decide to find out about the writer of the *Raj Quartet*. I dip into Hilary Spurling's biography *Paul Scott: A Life* and discover a surprisingly interesting question at the heart of the book. Why did Scott fall so completely in love with India when he was sent there on an Army posting in 1943? On first impressions he was an unlikely candidate to do that. But as with most of us, the clues to his preoccupations are in his upbringing, and Spurling untangles them meticulously. He was raised in the North London suburbs where everyone understood about social standing and neighbours exercised forensic analysis in judging one another's behaviour. Did you let your children play in the street? Did you eat in the kitchen? What did you wear when you went to the shops? Most people knew where they stood in the social hierarchy but his family occupied an uncomfortable position – neither middle class like his father nor working class like his mother and so he grew up feeling an outsider. It is perhaps this that made him so acutely aware of the Indian caste and class systems, and the ranked order of the British Army. It makes me think of my parents. My mother determinedly middle class in so many ways, and my father clinging to his working-class roots. She never forgave him for denying her the one thing she really wanted – to join the property-owning classes.

As promised, the scenery is stunning although I'm surprised that the colours are so muted. This is not a *Monsoon Wedding*. This is an altogether different and more serious story of India. Instead of bright swirling saris there are dusty landscapes and a great deal of khaki-coloured clothing. I'm not surprised to discover that the word khaki comes from the Urdu for dust.

My sympathies are mostly with the Indian characters, trapped and manipulated by imperialism. But the British characters face different traps. They and their forebears have been taught to believe that Britain was doing honourable work in India. Now they must come to terms with a new story, one that puts the plundering of resources at its livid centre. What was good? What was misguided? What was sheer exploitation? Even the word loot is stolen from the Hindi word lut! And they must face the impending loss of the way of life that they know and understand. They may not want to do it but they have no option.

I know these things are not easy.

Conundrums

Molly slips on a black and white furry jacket and squints in the hall mirror, carefully brushing on her mascara. 'What are you doing today?' she asks. It's Saturday morning and she's off to meet friends and do some shopping. Her social life is blooming.

'I'm not sure,' I say. I'm still adjusting to the novelty of having spare time after years of being a domestic fulcrum. And then, because I don't want her to worry that I'm lonely or adrift –

'I might make a start on learning how to do cryptic crosswords.'

'That's nice.' She frowns, grabs her bag and kisses my cheek. 'Have lots of fun! I'll see you tonight.'

I was full of enthusiasm when I added *The One With The Cryptic Crosswords* to the list. All my adult life they've annoyed and baffled me and I would love to be in on the joke with that select club of enthusiasts who chuckle smugly and swap clever clue solutions. But writing something on a list is the simple part and unlike some of the more straightforward treats I've ignored this one. In principle it should be easy as there's no shortage of material – every day brings a fresh crop of newspaper crosswords. On the other hand, I'm apprehensive as I might discover that I'm not very clever.

Today is the day to find out. I unfold my newspaper on the kitchen table and get started. I stare at it. And drink a lot of coffee.

Then I remember that yesterday's newspaper is in the recycling basket so I spread it out next to today's one which has the solutions. Working backwards may not be the intended way to do a crossword but it does provide a few aha! moments. I can see how to get from *First male worker is resolute* to *adamant*. But others leave me baffled. How does *Wrong actor tackling Romeo* lead to the solution *harm*?

I give up on that, have a solitary sandwich and then walk to Waterstones to look for a Teach Yourself Crosswords book. The one I choose guarantees to enlighten and provide confidence, and as I'm queuing to pay for it, I flick through the pages and learn that the first modern crossword was credited to a Liverpudlian journalist named Arthur Wynne. It was published in a New York newspaper in 1913 and he called it a word-cross but within just a few weeks it had settled into its familiar name due to a typesetting error. Early crosswords were of the simple definition variety and it wasn't until the 1920s in the UK that cryptic crosswords started to appear with each clue a puzzle in itself. They grew increasingly sophisticated and are still called British-style puzzles in the US.

Over the next few weeks, I have a couple of sessions of Teach-Myself though it's all rather dry and I don't look forward to them. Not for the first time I remind myself that treats aren't meant to be hard work.

I give up on the book plan and start looking around to see if there's a crossword course I could do. There's nothing. But this does nudge me closer to a solution as I realise that what I'm missing is having other people to learn with. My lone attempts haven't allowed for questions, laughs and distracting chat. I think about which of my friends do crosswords, and remember Caroline. When we used to work together, I'd often hear her discussing clues with like-minded colleagues. She's retired now but we've remained friends and the next time we meet for lunch in our local Fenwicks, I ask, 'Could you give me six Cryptic Crossword Masterclasses?' She looks taken aback to be cast as an expert, but when I explain my struggles, she quickly agrees. 'What fun!' she says and we settle on Thursday morning sessions at her house.

The following week I drive down the quiet lane that leads to Wisteria Cottage. When Caroline and I shared chatty coffee breaks at work, we discovered that we both grew up in Devon, although she was a couple of decades ahead of me. Gradually we heard about, and then met, key characters in one another's lives, and when I was devastated by Shaun's leukaemia, she was kind and supportive. The dips and dives of his illness tossed our family around – through the shock of diagnosis, a promising response to gene therapy drugs, resistance to those drugs, a search for a stem cell donor, high-dose chemotherapy, a stem cell infusion, complications, the agonies of Guillain-Barré Syndrome, a tumour on his hip, radiotherapy, and more stem cells. Then eventually after five years came the happy day when his consultant sat us down in her consulting room, the one we had both come to know so well, and told us that the latest tests had not detected any cancer cells and so she felt able – tentatively – to give him a good prognosis. Like so many of those who rode the waves with us, Caroline was perplexed by his decision to end our marriage just a few months later.

My friend puts the kettle on and once we've had a brief, efficient update on family news, we broach the subject of crosswords. In front of her is a pile of puzzles cut out from recent editions of The Daily Telegraph. I'm touched that she has prepared so well for her unsolicited role.

'The first thing you must do is learn to ignore the surface meaning,' she says. 'It's deliberately misleading. Instead, you look for the signs that tell you what kind of clue it is. We'll start with anagrams. You might want to take some notes here.'

I scribble away as she tells me that crossword setters have many ways of indicating that a group of letters need to be rearranged – the clue might include words or phrases, such as take apart, broken up, messed up, otherwise, different, reformed, inside out, split, upset, cooked, or brew. 'Here's a good one,' she says handing me a grid. *I leave guy floundering in a prestigious academic group (3,6).* 'The word floundering tells us that the solution is an anagram, so try rearranging the letters of I leave guy.'

I write them down. Then like magic, I see the answer – Ivy League – a neat fit for *prestigious academic group* which is the definition part of the clue.

'We'll do hidden words today, as well,' says Caroline. 'Look at this one.' *Battle ensued engulfing Prime Minister (6).* I rack my brains to think of a Prime Minister who bears the name of a battle. Churchill? Thatcher? McMillan? Peel? Wilson? I offer them all up without much conviction. She shakes her head. 'Attlee?' I say hopefully. At least it's the right number of letters. 'Yes!' she shouts. 'It's engulfed within the words *battle ensued*.'

Here's another one. *Feature of street in stockbroker belt (4).* I get that one straight away – kerb. Solving a clue brings a rush of pleasure. By the end of the morning, we've drunk a large pot of coffee, munched through a plate of biscuits and laughed a great deal. I've also made lots of notes and go home clutching a grid that Caroline has given me to look at before our next session.

She favours The Daily Telegraph crossword, which is a classic of the genre, and was used to recruit Allied codebreakers for the Enigma machine during the War – the fastest of the bunch all completed it within a deadline of twelve minutes. I'm keen to show off to myself so at the weekend I sit down to do my homework. My bravado is short lived. I spot one anagram and then sit disconsolately for half an hour.

'Don't worry a bit,' says Caroline when I confess. 'We've only just started. There are *hundreds* of conventions to learn.' In this second session, we move on to other tricks and fill in more solutions as she encourages me to think laterally. For *A well-oiled lock (5)*, she steers me away from my initial thoughts of keys, grease and latches. These are all too obvious. 'Think of another kind of lock,' she prompts and eventually we get to hair, and the solution which is *quiff*.

I like that one, and feel I am beginning – just beginning – to make some headway in this world where a flower can be a river, and butter can mean a ram or a goat.

Unexpected benefits

Caroline and I carry on with our sessions – I'm definitely making progress and am solving more clues with fewer prompts. But life outside of these pleasant diversions continues to deliver some unpleasant lurches and I arrive for our fifth session, feeling distracted. It's been a bad week, trying to negotiate some outstanding financial details from the divorce and as always, these days, Shaun and I are each unable to make sense of what the other wants. I'm hoping to put this human puzzle on one side today and concentrate instead on the difficult, but soluble cryptic variety.

When Caroline asks how things have been, it all spills out. I trust her. After Shaun left, I regularly spent afternoons in her garden, surrounded by roses and lilac as she handed me tea, tissues and home-made cake. My crying was at odds with the peaceful environment. It was snotty and snorty, and my apologies were incoherent. Many people find it hard to sit with someone who is distressed but my friend was steady. She didn't make herself feel better by jumping in with advice about what she would do. And she didn't fill the silences. She listened and she gave me her time.

This time she listens again. Attempting to disentangle thirty years of entwined financial affairs is stressful. But it's not until I talk it through that I realise the source of my upset is not the equity of pensions but the dangerous chill where once there was warmth. And later it strikes me that there are parallels here with cryptic crosswords. In the clue *A proper sort of pink flower (8)* you start out thinking you're in peony or foxglove territory but then you realise that you should be thinking about a yellow flower not a pink one because the answer is *primrose*.

By the next session I've untangled a few knots. I feel lighter and while we're poring over clues, Caroline's husband, Peter comes in and greets me with a warm hug. He asks after the children and enquires cheerfully about crossword progress. It's a second marriage for both of them. They were each divorced and had tough times but they survived and things got better.

As agreed at the start, our sixth session is the final one. 'You've passed with flying colours,' says Caroline. 'Keep on practising and you'll carry on improving. And remember you can always ask me if you're stuck.'

I am, at this point, still unable to finish a crossword unaided but I can at least appreciate the ingenuity of many of the clues. *Cool stall selling marine produce? (11)* is a satisfying one (standoffish). And the double definition variety is invariably pleasing. This toys with words that have more than one meaning such as *The bench come to a decision (6)* (settle), and *Saving a place for notices (8)* (hoarding). But with *Lingerie perhaps for parts of chest (7)*, I am distracted as no doubt the compiler intended, by bras and bodices until a few prompts get me back on the path that leads to drawers.

I've enjoyed these masterclasses enormously but it's the added benefits of friendship that have turned them into a real treat. Caroline is kind, tactful and genuine. That's her friendship style and I always feel better for seeing her.

Later in the week, I meet another friend, Frances, in a low-beamed, cosy pub. She, too, is generous and listens but she adds a different piece to the puzzle by challenging me to reframe things, and not to stick with the victim narrative. She reminds me that it wasn't just Shaun, who was unhappy and wanted to end things – as we grew further apart, I'd become miserable too. It's uncomfortable to hear but it helps me move forward.

We talk, too, about trust and the muddled collection of fears that are getting in the way of my feelings towards Mike. Is it possible to have a happy relationship? Can *I* have a happy relationship? Will I always feel second best? Our break was only brief. It was never intended to be permanent but it was enough to know for sure that I missed him. 'He's lovely,' she says. 'Enjoy it and be grateful.' It's a gift to have friends with whom I can be vulnerable. And I want them to feel the same about me. If we don't share our imperfect selves with others, how can we know that it's normal to get angry, to get frustrated with our children or to feel jealous?

When I put cryptic crosswords on my list, I didn't anticipate that it would turn out to be such a sociable activity. And the crossword companionship continues. A couple of weeks after finishing my masterclasses I set off on the train to Leicester to visit Rick and Claire for the weekend. They are new friends that I've met through Mike, and I like them very much. I buy a newspaper for the journey, scan the headlines and turn quickly to the crossword. As usual, it appears impenetrable at first. But a train journey is just what I need – the luxury of uninterrupted time when I can worry away at the clues – and by the time I arrive I've solved a third of them.

Mike meets me at the station and as I spot him, my heart skips – his face is creased by deep laughter lines that stretch from the corners of his eyes to his cheeks.

The next morning, I remember that my hosts are cryptic fans, so I fish out my crossword and together we sit in the garden and finish it. Then they produce their favoured puzzle, the Saturday Guardian. This turns out to be quite different from the Telegraph, and more inclined to be lewd. All weekend, in between trips out, chatting, and eating food that tastes delicious because someone else has chosen and cooked it, we return to the crossword. We groan at the puns and occasionally, just occasionally, I solve a clue myself. It's taken a while but at long last I'm in on the joke. At long last I'm a member of the club.

Old ways, new ways

It's turning out to be a beautiful summer, and on my visits to see Mike we often end up driving to Dorset. There are glorious beaches there including Studland, with its history of naturism stretching back to the 1920s. I love this new-found freedom and the feel of the sun all over me.

We've discovered, too, that we share an enthusiasm for architecture. We're both untutored but curious and it's a new interest to explore together. And so, one afternoon, with sand between our toes, on our way back from the beach, I pluck a treat from my list and we stop off at Poundbury. This is the experimental model village on the outskirts of Dorchester that was commissioned by Charles as Prince of Wales, and has been developed with 'keen endorsement' from him, on land owned by the Duchy of Cornwall. A core aim is to create a community with housing, shops and businesses where people don't have to rely on driving. Building began in 1993 and continues, with the ultimate intention of having 2,500 houses and a population of 6,000. I've long been intrigued by the idea of developing a community from nothing, and want to see it for myself.

The first thing that surprises me when we arrive is the silence. It's broken by just two sounds. We hear a child's screams coming from inside a dental surgery. And the pavements are covered in pebbles which make a satisfying Georgian crunch as we walk on them.

The other surprise is that the houses are mostly mock-Georgian or mock-Victorian. Some even have bricked-up windows aping real old buildings and their attempts to avoid paying tax on windows. In the *eighteenth* century!

The principles are sound – architectural harmony, local building materials, size on a human scale, and avoiding unnecessary signs. I can't disagree with those. The thread running back to the past provides stability. And yet it feels inauthentic. An aching for the past when there's already so much of the real past in England. I'd like to see Charles championing new designs. Less overtly safe but still with solid human values. Showing some confidence in modern architecture.

The website doesn't help. It tells me that this development is quite unlike anywhere else…and that many people describe Poundbury as like visiting a living film-set.

At the moment everything looks new and perfect. Too perfect until I spot a building that has signs of weathering. Never have I been so pleased to see walls with spreading rust marks and damp. They make a small corner look real.

The philosopher Alain de Botton is characteristically clear in his verdict. 'Poundbury captures the spirit of eighteenth-century country life but is psychologically disconnected from contemporary society. Maddening, like an elderly relative to whom you were close when you were a child but who lacks any understanding of the adult you have become, shaped by circumstances for better or worse.'

It's easy to mock but there *are* things I like. The proportions are pleasing and the streets run at unexpected angles to one another adding surprise and interest. They're curved in order to calm traffic and dissuade driving. And the buildings have been designed and constructed with energy efficiency in mind.

After a walk around the village, we finish up with tea and scones at a cafe painted in tasteful Farrow and Ball tones. We're the only people there and so it's particularly noticeable when we linger…and linger, chewing over our impressions. Agreeing. Disagreeing. Listening. Reconsidering. We order a second pot of tea. And then at last the waitress tells us that they will be locking up soon and so we need to leave. Later, as my head hits the pillow and I replay what we did today, I think happily about this – our chat in the cafe. It was my favourite part of the day.

Golden tickets

It's been such a long time since 1980 when I last went to a music festival. The Beach Boys were headlining at Knebworth, and two years earlier I'd spent my first pay packet on a bulky Sanyo music centre. It had a smoky black lid and brittle plastic hinges and was my most treasured possession. I lived in London with friends and a stack of vinyl, and went to as many gigs as I could. Music was fun. It was essential. It was always there.

And then it wasn't.

The music didn't die in one American Pie-like day, but I got married at twenty-four and Shaun didn't share my enthusiasm so I gradually stopped using it for that instant fix of joy that I once took for granted. Other things seemed more important. We were working hard at being grown-ups and creating lives different from those of our parents. Shaun's childhood scarred by boarding school at seven and his mother's mental illness – mine by the fears, frustrations and disappointments of my parents. Adult life was the Promised Land and after only a few years we managed to buy a small flat in South London. The kitchen floorboards had rotted away leaving great holes, and we didn't have enough money for repairs, so for months we leapt from one side to the other. Shaun was in the final stage of his legal training and I had just started work on a PhD.

We stayed in London for another decade, moving on up the housing ladder. But by the time we had three children, we longed for a bigger garden, a dog, a small primary school and a gentler pace of life so we began spending Saturdays on house-hunting expeditions to Sussex. I envisaged a practical house in a village, near to a train station as Shaun would have to commute. But we ended up with something very different and that laid the foundations for a completely new lifestyle. What happened was that Shaun and eight-year-old Will lost their hearts to a little house, miles down an overgrown lane. It included a chunk of land and they were enchanted by the bluebell wood and rare orchids. It wasn't what I'd had in mind but with a bit of persuasion, I quelled my misgivings and once it was ours, resolved to get on with using the fields and raising happy children.

Years flashed by – we had another baby, and all too soon I was forty-something with four children at four different schools. Our rural dreamscape was a large unruly garden, tangled woods, two fields, a great deal of time in the car, an oppressive mortgage as we had by then extended the house – and a menagerie.

Shaun commuted to his job as a solicitor in London and I was in charge of the dogs, chickens, geese, goats, pigs, cats, lambs, guinea pigs, and children. In the morning before the school run, I would lead our two goats across a field to the woods where they would browse contentedly all day among the brambles. In the evening, I would bring them back to their shed in the garden and lock them up for the night. That was the plan but sometimes life didn't go smoothly and I'd get distracted and forget to collect them. Then I'd wake up in the small hours and lie there feeling guilty. Goats hate getting cold and wet, so eventually my conscience would propel me into my wellies and dressing gown, across the dark field and through the gate by the stream. There, Gwyneth and Mirabel would appear from among the shadowy, moonlit trees, sweetened by curiosity. What inevitably followed was a merry dance as I attempted to attach them to my rope and they did their best to trip me up.

I loved being a wife and mum and gave thanks for my good fortune. But the relentless, rain-sodden, resource-draining reality was a challenge. I don't like mud, goats and chaos now and I didn't like those things then. Somehow, I'd become a woman who spent her time trimming goats' hooves, clipping chickens' wings, restraining pigs, and bottle-feeding lambs. I felt a surprised pride in doing these things, but they were not part of the me I expected to be.

Throughout all of this, I believed fiercely that by hard work and determination I could make a loving marriage and a happy family. But what I did not understand was that sometimes snakes slither into life's folds, unbidden.

Now I want some fun.

When I made my list, the Glastonbury Festival was one of the first things that came to mind – wanting to see what all the fuss is about and longing for a few carefree days. At that time, I was in the final months of my marriage to Shaun – though I didn't know that then – and I had no idea when or with whom, I might go. It wouldn't have appealed to him. I would have had to justify. To answer the question 'Why do you want to do that?'

Luckily Mike's as keen to go as I am. After all, it *is* the largest greenfield performing arts festival in the world.

And therein lies a problem as unlike most of the treats I can't just decide to do it. I have to get hold of some tickets. I've already tried once – in 2012 when I was newly separated and planning to go with Henry and Molly. We went through the preliminary hurdles of registering and getting photo ID. Then at 9am on an October Sunday morning when the phone lines opened, we were on our mobiles and landline, dialling and redialling. 'It's like trying to get through to God,' complained Henry. After an hour and forty minutes, the website informed us that all tickets were now sold.

The next year things were different. Mike and I joined in an extended family effort to all get tickets for one another – you can buy eight at a time. We were scattered across the country and after fifty minutes, Emma texted to say that they'd struck lucky and the rest of the group would now try to get tickets for us. Her boyfriend's sister's boyfriend managed to get through and by the end of the morning we had a date in our diary for June.

In the intervening months we mentioned it to various friends and acquaintances – some shared our excitement and others looked horrified. 'All that mud,' they shuddered, '…and the toilets. No *thank you!*'

Now it's summer and with just a few weeks to go, Emma's boyfriend's sister's boyfriend – who we've still not met – passes on a list of useful things to take to a festival. We can safely ignore the condoms but we gather up wellies, hats, antibacterial hand gel, earplugs, waterproofs, toilet rolls, camping chairs, camping pillows, glitter, and a borrowed tent. I pack some wafty long dresses and a headband of pale pink roses. At long last, it's here and I'm ready for some fun.

Dancing in the dark

It's a Wednesday afternoon in June and we've just driven into a vast field where a series of young men and women in shorts and wellies direct us to a parking spot. We join row upon row of cars, many adorned with paper flowers and rainbow stickers and as I turn the engine off, the space next to us is taken by a small hatchback car. We stare at the young woman who climbs out, giggling and pulling at her short white dress. When she straightens up, we see that she is also wearing a long veil and white wellies. Festival fancy dress maybe? Her travelling companion unfolds his long body from the car. He's in grey shorts and a grey T-shirt with peacock-green trainers. He gazes adoringly at the young woman and can't stop smiling. All doubt is dispelled when three adult bridesmaids appear. Flower fairies in short, frothy, purple dresses. We join in the general delight, add our congratulations to the new couple, and take a few photos. Then we unpack the car and start the long walk down a high-hedged lane to the camp site and the boiled-sweet-striped tents in the distance.

Our home is a basic tent, and once it's set up, we wander around the site. The music programme doesn't get going till Friday but there's plenty to see – masks; face paint; bowler hats; grass skirts; furry animal outfits; wellies wellies wellies spotted, striped and plain; false beards; flashing sunglasses;

inflatable sofas; frayed shorts; suntanned thighs; bandanas; fire eaters; hippie outfits; sexy outfits; milkmaid outfits; carefully accessorised outfits; thrown together outfits; barely-there-outfits; hula hoops; flower circlets; tipis; toe-wiggling babies; screaming toddlers; love, peace... and everyone with the non-negotiable ID lanyard. Overstimulated, we stop for drinks in a fantasy fairy dell.

By Friday lunchtime when we see Blondie, with Debbie Harry still glamorous in her late sixties and tottering around in terrifically high heels – she was never known for her dancing – I've developed a taste for festival food and the silliness of silent discos. Later, we watch Arcade Fire in the dark. Just a few bars in and the crowd roars with collective euphoria. I'm right in the middle.

Next afternoon we're wandering through the vast site when we come across a large group of men, women and children dressed as insects with spindly stilts, copper-coloured body paint and strange metal eyes. It's all going well until they get muddled up with a Punjabi marching band. Then we go to a forties-themed tea tent and as we're eating our Victoria sponge, the waitresses – all floral sprigged dresses and Victory-roll hair – break into an Andrews Sisters song and dance routine.

All of that leaves us feeling exhausted and so we climb up the hill to the giant patchwork letters that spell out Glastonbury. From a relatively quiet patch of grass, we can look down on everything and take a nap in the sunshine. The cone of Glastonbury Tor is just a few miles away. It was once on an island surrounded by the marshlands of the Somerset Levels and depending on your point of view, this is where Joseph of Arimathea brought his young nephew, Jesus, in pursuit of his interests in tin mining...where he came with the Holy Grail, the cup used by Jesus at the Last Supper...where he founded England's first church...where King Arthur's sword Excalibur was forged...where Arthur was brought after being wounded in battle... Before we came, I'd wondered if it was coincidence that the festival sprouted on a well-established farm so near to a site of spiritual significance. It's not.

Back in 1971 some rich hippies were looking for a site with sacred significance where they could stage a celebration of spiritual awakening and a demonstration against corporate greed. Their first choice was Stonehenge but it wasn't suitable as the surrounding crop fields would be at their peak in June. Then they were put in touch with Michael Eavis, a young farmer who had recently inherited Worthy Farm from his parents and was struggling to survive. It was just seven miles from Glastonbury Tor with all its myths and legends and even better, he was a music lover and had already held his own small festival at the farm. It was a great match. Arabella Churchill and her friends got to work organising their festival, dousing the area for ley lines and creating an area where alien spaceships could land if they happened to be passing. The headline act was David Bowie. It was just one week after his first performance on *Top of the Pops* and everything ran so late that it was dawn before he played. He was by all accounts both spectacular and high on mushrooms.

Refreshed by our nap and a walk, we sit on the ground in a tent to watch *Beggars of Life* – a silent Louise Brooks classic – while Mark Kermode's band the Dodge Brothers provides a live musical accompaniment. It's brilliant. The film is poignant and funny with heavy eye make-up, exaggerated expressions and darty movements. Then we watch a couple of circus acts with trapeze artists high in the air, wearing fixed grins as they twirl round scarlet drapes. On our way to see Bryan Ferry we pass a podium packed with people dancing. Many are dressed as mermaids and other sea creatures. I have a quick whirl and make myself dizzy. Later, we chat to someone who asks, 'Did I see you dancing on stage with a prawn?'

'Yes that's right,' I say.

Bryan Ferry is lizard-cool in leather trousers and after that we dance to pulsating electronic music in a field. The focus is a colossal mechanical spider made of cranes from Southampton Docks. It spews coloured flames high into the black and silver sky. The grass is cool and damp under my feet. No-one cares what I do, what I wear or that I always dance on the offbeat. We both love it and stay to the end.

On the slow, sleepy wander back to our tent we stumble through disturbing post-apocalyptic installations, then we pass three female fire-eaters and an enclosure of huge mechanical creatures made from parts of tractors, motorbikes and combine harvesters. One has a horse-shaped head and another, great wings like a Pteranodon. Their headlights beam through the dark as they dance to Rolling Stones classics.

On Sunday afternoon we find a place near the back of a massive throng. It reminds me of the Sermon on the Mount scene in Monty Python's Life of Brian. We're all here to welcome Dolly Parton to the now traditional Legends slot that has helped to reignite the careers of Johnny Cash, Tom Jones and Tony Bennett. I've never thought of myself as a country fan but her personality dazzles like her rhinestones. She's very funny and it's impossible not to be charmed.

In the evening, we pack up our tent and slip out to avoid the crush when everyone leaves tomorrow. We're back to being sensible but this weekend I rediscovered a room that had been locked for years. The door creaked open. I forgot all those worries about where my life is going. I spread out my arms and I danced.

Not guilty

Unlike many of our friends, Shaun and I didn't have doting grandparents nearby who could help out when we longed for a break. But just occasionally when we were still living in London, he would take the children to see his mother in Somerset and I would get a weekend to myself. Those rare days would be filled with pleasures like knowing my hairbrush was where I last left it, and pursuing a thought to its conclusion. I'd go for walks, eat simple food and curl up on the sofa to watch a film or two. Or three. Best of all were old Hollywood ones.

Other times I'd take the children and stay with my sister so that Shaun could have some time to himself. He looked forward to these breaks like I did but there was one weekend when it all went wrong. He'd decided to spend Saturday at an exhibition about sustainable housebuilding and on the way there he called in at his office. Unfortunately, the lift jammed while he was in it, and as he couldn't get any kind of mobile signal and no-one else was at work, it took a couple of hours to attract attention. It was early afternoon by the time he was free to set off for Olympia. When he got there, he was surprised to see a large number of dark-skinned men milling around outside, chatting and looking cheerful. He couldn't identify their language and assumed, somewhat mystified, that sustainable housebuilding must be popular in their community. Eventually as he waited for tickets, someone explained that he was a week early and currently in the queue for a Tamil conference. When we spoke that evening, he was *thoroughly* cross and *thoroughly* unhappy. And I felt *thoroughly* guilty to be having fun with the children.

He was cross and unhappy a lot. And I felt guilty a lot.

There was a smorgasbord of things that made me feel guilty including:

> *Not having a thrusting career like Shaun*
>
> *Not having to commute on rammed, unreliable trains like Shaun*
>
> *Feeling I was neglecting Shaun when I gave the children attention*
>
> *Feeling I was neglecting the children when I gave Shaun attention*
>
> *Longing to have some time to myself but feeling that meant I was a bad mother*
>
> *When I had time to myself, feeling that I was neglecting both Shaun and the children*

I don't recall Shaun expressing guilt about *anything*.

So why was *I* riddled with it? It's another of those mysteries that I can revisit with hindsight. It might cast some light on how I got to where I am now. And if I know *that*, then I might be able to steer a better course out of my confusion about what I want.

Maternal guilt, I used to think. It goes with the job. But recently I was staying with a friend in Birmingham and while we were having a relaxed post-breakfast chat about life and families, she inadvertently provided a more nuanced explanation. 'The thing is,' she said, 'I'm a people pleaser. Always have been…still am I suppose…like a lot of women.' There was a pause while I rubbed my thumb back and forth around the rim of my coffee mug, and processed this idea.

'Me too!' I said. 'I've never thought of it that way but now you've said it, then it's obvious.' And I remembered what another friend used to say when we were swapping tales of maternal frustration – 'You're only ever as happy as your least happy child.'

'Or husband,' I would mutter. Like her I'd do almost anything to preserve family harmony motivated by a genuine desire for the well-being of my loved ones – as well as an undeniable quest for a quiet life. Without realising, though, I fell into the trap of measuring my worth against how happy Shaun and the children were. With five people to keep happy I spent a lot of time doing what I thought everyone else wanted and a lot of time feeling that it wasn't going well.

It's risky being a people pleaser. It's easy to lose sight of who you are and what you need. And I can't blame anyone else. I did it to myself.

So, if I could go back and do it all again would I do it differently? Because I still wonder why we spent so much time and money on our menagerie. Maybe we were both in a conspiracy to keep one another happy. Me thinking that Shaun wanted to retreat home to the rural good life after a stressful day in the City, him thinking I found animal husbandry fulfilling as part of some traditional fantasy, and us both wanting the children to have the kind of storybook childhood neither of us had. But these choices could only be made without the benefit of hindsight. And there *was* plenty that was good. It was fun at times and when it wasn't, it provided a stock of family stories. We all enjoy the memory of our high-and-mighty neighbour waving her rake ineffectually as our delighted pig munched his way through her herbaceous border.

It's telling, though, that when I made my list, it did not include any animal-related activities – nothing that involved slipping around in the mud chasing stubborn goats, mending fences, or coaxing orphaned lambs to stay alive. Instead, there were a couple of film-related treats. Exactly the kind of thing that I chose to do when I had those precious weekends in the past. *Watch Billy Wilder's films* is on the list. I know a few already and am partial to his acerbic dialogue and depiction of post-war America and Europe. Now I want to see them all.

This project has stretched out over some months and I haven't watched in any particular order. I started with *Avanti!* which is the slight but satisfying story of an American who travels to an Italian island and discovers that his father had a secret life there. Played by Jack Lemmon and Juliet Mills against a backdrop of gorgeous Mediterranean scenery, it was perfect escapism for a quiet evening on my own.

Since then, there have been many quiet evenings and afternoons on my own and now I've finished all twenty-six. He was a versatile director, tackling romantic comedies, farce, satire, tragedy and even a musical. His breakthrough movie, *Double Indemnity*, was released in 1944 and is considered by many critics to be the greatest example of film noir. When Hitchcock saw it, he said, 'The two most important words in Hollywood are Billy and Wilder,' and by the time he died aged 95 he had received a total of six Oscars for directing and screenwriting.

He often contrasts the brashness of American life with sophisticated European ways and he was well-qualified to do this because he was born in Vienna, to a Jewish family, and started his career as a reporter both there and in Berlin, before fleeing to the US. As a director he attracted the biggest stars of the day including Humphrey Bogart, James Stewart, and Walter Matthau. Audrey Hepburn is adorable in both *Love in the Afternoon* and *Sabrina*, and Marilyn Monroe sparkles in *Some Like It Hot* and *The Seven-Year Itch* despite being difficult to direct. She frequently fluffed her lines but Wilder said, 'I always forgave her…Marilyn was never on time. Not once. Of course, I have an old aunt in Vienna who was always on time to everything but who would want to see her in a movie?'

It's not original to say that *Some Like It Hot* is my favourite but then it *is* almost universally agreed to be brilliant. *Ace in the Hole*, on the other hand, is an intriguing discovery – the story of a cynical reporter who tries to advance his own career by delaying the rescue of a man trapped in a cave. In its day it was considered a failure, but today it ranks highly amongst critics and was way ahead of its time in tackling press immorality. My other favourites are *Double Indemnity, Love in the Afternoon, Sabrina, The Lost Weekend, Sunset Boulevard*, and *The Spirit of St. Louis*. All of these were made in the forties and fifties when Hollywood elegance was at its height. What *did* give me pause for thought was the 1942 film, *The Major and the Minor*, where Ginger Rogers's character is broke and hits upon the idea of disguising herself as a 12-year-old so she can get a half-price ticket home from New York. On the train, the conductor sees her smoking and becomes suspicious so she tries to avoid him by hiding in the compartment of an Army major played by

Ray Milland. He can't quite figure out why he's attracted to such a young girl but although he is perfectly well-behaved, the subject matter seems inappropriate nowadays and makes me uncomfortable.

I enjoy *The Apartment* from 1960, but some of the later films seem coarser and gaudier and these are the ones I like least. At the bottom of my list are *The Private Life of Sherlock Holmes*, and *Fedora*, with a special mention for *Irma La Douce* because I find Shirley MacLaine so irritating.

I could, it is true, have happily missed out on *The Emperor Waltz*, a lightweight musical set in the court of the Austrian emperor with lovelorn dogs, dancing Tyrolean peasants and Bing Crosby in lederhosen. But even this – generally considered to be his worst film – is old-fashioned escapism and a pleasant enough way to spend a few hours in the cause of completeness.

So, thank you Billy Wilder. It's been a treat – many hours in the company of great actors, sharp dialogue and some thought-provoking plots.

And it's all been guilt-free.

Just a jacket

It's not unreasonable to expect that with middle age comes greater insight and wisdom. After all, the more you live, the more you can look back on your story and try to make some sense of it. I now know that people-pleasing was one of the biggest traps that ensnared me and no doubt will continue to do so, although maybe I'm better equipped to spot it these days. But we humans set all kinds of traps for ourselves and I keep finding new ones that trip me up. And so, unlikely as it sounds, that's what happened with my knitting treat.

I love knitting. Its name comes from the Old English *cnyttan* meaning to tie in a knot, and there's something magical about creating wonderful textures and patterns simply by taking a ball of wool and twisting it into knots. And then there's the satisfaction that comes from making sense of the strange knitting pattern language. It is impenetrable to the uninitiated, so much so that people were banned from sending knitting patterns abroad during World War Two in case they contained coded messages. Another benefit of knitting is that it's extremely relaxing. I can't quite manage to knit while walking along as people did in the Middle Ages but for me the rhythmic clicking and clacking is the perfect accompaniment to an evening in front of the television. It is soothing and also helps to stop me from falling asleep which I generally do as soon as I sit down and get comfortable.

'A jacket to wear over jeans – that would be useful,' I thought and put it on my list. It was one of the first treats I started and so it is now several years since I chose some fuchsia-pink wool and a stylish pattern in rice stitch, already imagining friends admiring my professional-looking, new accessory. For several months, I knitted industriously. And optimistically. And had no trouble in telling myself that the front, back and sleeves looked quite good. But I'd conveniently put previous knitting tribulations out of my mind and when I got to the tedious sewing-up stage, it all went wrong. The best word I could find to describe my new jacket was lumpy. Disappointed, I stuffed it in a drawer and tried to ignore it.

About three months later I was keen to try again and this time I used a slightly finer yarn in sensible navy blue. It started off well and was looking promising. But then life got complicated... I lost the motivation...and eventually I lost the pattern.

Quite a few months passed without any knitting, and then my fingers grew restless and I felt ready for a new project. So I made a trip to a haberdashery shop and after much enjoyable deliberation returned home with a pattern for a short, collared jacket, and some soft Air Force blue wool. There may have been some hiccups with this particular treat but this time I knew it was going to be different.

For weeks I clicked away, contented and relaxed, until at last I had all the necessary sections waiting to be assembled. I pressed ahead with the sewing-up, keeping my thoughts focused on the end product and quashing any doubts.

Eventually it was ready and I put it on. I tried as hard as I could to welcome it into my life but it wasn't good. It turned out that Air Force blue just isn't my colour. And like its predecessor, it was a bit lumpy. 'I'll give it a wash,' I thought. 'Maybe that will help.' So, I put it in the washing machine.

It came out toddler-sized.

I was so disheartened that I decided to give up on my knitting project. After all I'd tried, and that in itself was worthy of a tick.

But now many months have passed, and I can no longer ignore the niggling feeling that something is missing. So once again I set off for the haberdashery shop full of hope. This time I opt for a long loose jacket in random greens and purples. Colours that suit me better than Air Force blue. And a good shape for disguising vital evidence in the *Does My Bum Look Big In This* debate.

The pattern does indeed keep me awake through many hours of TV watching and the more tense the plot, the faster my needles go. The knitting stage is completed quicker than I would like and then there's nothing left but to press the pieces and sew them together.

I wish I could report a happy ending.

For all of my adult life, I've knitted. And I have nothing to show for it. Not one home-knitted item has secured a place in my wardrobe. Many years ago, I tried knitting children's clothes and made Will a beige round-necked pullover. It fitted well and I deemed it a success, but half-way through a second one – this time in maroon – I had a moment of doubt.

'You *will* wear it, won't you?' I asked.

'W-e-ll...' said Will, wriggling as he came up with what was an impressively tactful response for an eight-year-old. '...

perhaps I could wear it in the house.' So I tried making squares for blankets but that just resulted in an awful lot of sewing up and not so much knitting.

All of this leaves me with an uncomfortable question. How can I keep getting it so wrong?

Why do I not know myself well enough to recognise that I'm not good at knitting and don't seem to improve however much of it I do. Not to mention the all-important fact that I don't wear woollen jumpers or jackets as I'm nearly always too hot. If I ever do feel a bit chilly, I put on a non-lumpy Marks & Spencer cardigan.

Why? I could ask that about *so* many of the things I do. I've fallen into many traps over the years. This one is the dogged trap. Just keep doggedly ploughing on with the optimistic thought that it might work out. It might not be lumpy. It might fit. I might suddenly change my mind and like wearing wool. The problem in so many situations – relationships, jobs, ambitions, and yes, even knitting – is knowing when to call it a day.

And I mustn't forget the hormone trap. When biochemistry overrides good sense. For about a year after Molly was born, my hormones kept telling me 'You want another baby. You *do*. You *really do.*' But it was just an oxytocin rush and a reluctance to accept that my reproductive years were over. It would have been madness to have a fifth baby.

This trap is particularly relevant at the moment. I remember where I was when my friend Isla told me about her friend called Mike. I was sitting on the bottom stair with my phone attached to my ear. 'He was widowed three years ago,' she said. 'I think you'd get on. Can I put you in touch?'

'Hmm...' I said, taken off guard and mumbling about it only being nine months since I separated from Shaun, but how if I was going to date someone, I'd want them to have a sense of humour, generosity of spirit, curiosity about life, and an open mind.

'He has all of those in spades,' she said. 'And lovely eyes too.'

'OK,' I said. Then I got cold feet and told her not to take it any further. She ignored me and copied us in on an email, saying she hoped we would become friends. I could have ducked out at that stage but somewhere inside I still had a pilot light burning – with curiosity about relationships. So we went ahead and met up. Now eighteen months on I have to keep in mind the literary device that gives me such a jolt when I come across it in novels. I am an unreliable narrator for my own life. I must do my best not to misread what my poor love-addled brain is telling me.

Edging along in Berlin

It's turning into a busy summer. Mike and I are planning a few days away and as Berlin is on my list and neither of us has ever been, that's where we're going. Henry has finished his second year at university and Molly has just done her GCSEs so we've invited them to join us. It's the first time that they and Mike will have spent so much time together and I'm anxious about whether we'll all get on. It's a delicate stage. Attempting to stitch new relationships together. Starting out on a new relationship in mid-life is so much harder than when I met Shaun, and we were young, free to dream, and had less baggage. Now there are complicated loyalties and responsibilities and the potential for so much upset.

Berlin divides opinion. One friend recently returned from a visit enthusing about the arty vibes and interesting architecture. Another was overwhelmed and oppressed by its terrible history. And as we emerge from the subway station for our first breath of warm Berlin air we are immediately confronted by a reminder of dark times. We stumble through a small burial ground, dragging our cabin bags and Mike points to a headstone listing five names from one family. It's one of many dated May 1st 1945, right at the end of the war – when the Soviets battled for control of the city and thousands of Berliners were killed.

Our small apartment is in the eaves of a tall building that was formerly behind the Wall. It's simple but will suit us ideally as a base for a couple of days so we dump our bags, splash water on our faces, and set off in search of some lunch. The street is wide and busy and we quickly find a cafe where we can sit outside in the midsummer sunshine. Tattooed cyclists jingle past, perched upright, loosely connected to the handlebars. And at the tables on either side of us are pairs of young men, all in sharp waistcoats and with neat beards. They lean back, laugh and suck casually on their cigarettes.

Henry and Molly are on best behaviour, being polite and amenable. We all are – none of us wants to stand out as *the bossy one* so we've avoided making any plans so far. But as we tuck into our pizzas, we toss ideas around and agree that what we need is an introduction to the city's history. Several museums claim to offer this and the one we end up choosing is The Berlin Story – it's got great reviews and is housed inside a huge concrete bunker that was once an air raid shelter. Terrible facts are presented with unflinching honesty and in one room we come across the worst kind of list. It details the systematic erosion of Jewish rights under the Nazis.

In another room we read about Barbed Wire Sunday in August 1961, when East Berliners woke up to find a barbed wire barrier surrounding their sector of the city. A quarter of the population had already rejected the Soviet regime and left, but others were tethered by family, friends and community. Some couldn't bear to leave their loved ones' graves behind. Soon after, the Berlin Wall was built using concrete blocks, and rubble from wartime bomb sites. By then it was too late to escape. There were no phone lines to the West, people were recruited to spy on their community and family, and letters were opened by the security services. Where shops would once have proudly proclaimed family names, they were renamed in keeping with state ownership – food shop…meat shop…book shop. When we meet up in the cafe for tea and cherry tart, Henry and Molly are uncharacteristically quiet.

The next morning is given over to the Jewish Museum. We stare at ancient religious treasures and the final belongings of Holocaust victims, cradled here within architect Daniel Libeskind's brilliant building, designed to evoke feelings of oppression and loss. When viewed from above it looks like a broken Star of David. Inside, corridors run at oblique angles and the walls of the grey, dead-end Holocaust Tower have irregular window slits. To cross one passage, I have to trample across thousands of iron discs, cut like screaming faces with wide eyes and open mouths. Afterwards, as we walk towards the Reichstag and the Brandenburg Gate, we come across the Memorial to the Murdered Jews of Europe – a labyrinth of over 2,700 grey concrete slabs in varying heights. The layout is confusing and as we explore, trying to understand, we lose one another. When I realise they have disappeared I attempt to stay calm but my guts fizz and my heart thuds. I rush from alley to alley, searching – seeing other families in the distance but not my own. Eventually we are reunited. We are sobered and grateful.

For our final evening I've reserved a table at one of Berlin's dark restaurants. There are several of these, all temporarily depriving diners of their sense of sight so that other senses are heightened. Some do this by providing blindfolds but most create a dark environment. The one that I've booked claims to be 32% darker than all other dark restaurants…

As we get ready to go, I'm first in the bathroom – I shower, slip on a long blue and white cotton dress and strappy white sandals, and apply minimal makeup. Just a hopeful smile in fuchsia pink. I want this evening to go well. Ten minutes. Job done. Mike's quick too. Dark jeans over his long slim legs, and a soft purple V-neck over a T-shirt. Molly takes a great interest in clothes. She gets frustrated by my lack of interest but approves of Mike's casual but particular style.

I'm ready and so is Mike but Henry and Molly refuse to be hurried. Their hair and outfits require dedication. As a university lecturer, Mike spends a lot of time with young people. He knows how to talk to them but with no children of his own these essential sartorial preparations come as a surprise. He raises his voice impatiently, I jump up and down ineffectually, and Molly and Henry are indignant. We're *so* unreasonable.

We dash down the stairs and through the busy streets in a grumpy, breathless rush and arrive fifteen minutes late. But it's not a problem. The receptionist is welcoming and shows us into a dimly-lit bar where we calm down and order drinks. A barman hands out menus and tells us to choose one of the five options – beef, poultry, fish, vegetarian or surprise. Mike chooses vegetarian, Henry and Molly opt for fish and my choice is poultry. We can see from the printed menus that we'll be having four courses but the descriptions remind me of particularly impenetrable cryptic crossword clues. Mike's starter promises to provide 'a taste of Aztecan masculinity on wavy green and voluptuous red bedding' and I'm intrigued by my dessert. 'A dark beauty, illuminated by the delicate seduction and admiration of her rosy companions.'

All the waiters are blind or partially-sighted. Ours is Ben. He introduces himself, asks our names, and instructs us firmly in two basic rules. We are not to move around the restaurant on our own, and we must use no light source of any kind. This includes lighters, mobile phones and watches. Then we form a conga line and follow our leader round a corner until the outside world is banished and there is nothing but blackness. He guides us to a table and explains where our chairs are. I'm already disoriented and it takes a few seconds to work out whether I'm standing in front of my chair or behind.

We are now dependent on Ben and over the course of the next few hours, he takes good care of us, turning up periodically and speaking with practised care and clarity –

'Now Mike, I am passing the soup to you from the right. It's at shoulder height. Pass it on to Henry…'

'Imagine that your place setting is a clock. Your spoons are at twelve o'clock…'

At first, we eat in silence. The food is delicious but it's perplexing and requires concentration. I can tell that there is satay sauce in my starter, but other ingredients are elusive. Maybe something unusual like chicory? We swap samples, taking one another's hands and guiding them towards our plates, hesitating and debating what we might be tasting. The food is the focus without the usual distractions of looking at what the people at the next table are doing and wearing, and eavesdropping on what they are saying. We hear other people talking but the tables must be widely spaced as their speech sounds distant. At one point a bottle smashes to the ground.

There's a longish break between the first and second courses and to pass the time, I suggest a game. I ask everyone to name a place they love. Molly's is Chatsworth which she and I have recently visited together, and Henry chooses New York because of the jazz and the bustle. Mike enthuses about Johannesburg's vibrant modern African culture, and I offer up thirty-year old memories of sitting in an oceanside shack restaurant in Monterey, eating clam chowder and watching pelicans and sea otters. When we've all had our turn, we have another couple of rounds with music and films.

At the end, when we go into the light I see a big red stain down the front of my dress. This must be thanks to the rosy companions in my dessert. We've thoroughly enjoyed the food even though we didn't know what it was. Nor do we know what kind of room we've been in for the past few hours. Opulent? Colourful? Minimalist? Faded? We accepted what we were given and undistracted by our surroundings we all listened intently and learned new things about one another. Here in Berlin, we edged along in the dark. It was intense. It was fun and it was unforgettable.

Thorns

Modern Berlin is exciting and grown-up. It doesn't shy away from facing its history, and it's hard to believe that this city was enemy territory just fourteen years before I was born. But a big question remains at the end of this trip, and after we get home, I puzzle over it. I gnaw at it. I toss it up in the air like a bone.

And *still* it is a question in search of an answer. All of those collective injustices. All of those individual cruelties. All of that suffering enshrined in the museums and memorials. How did Berliners get on with their lives after that? Did they forgive? Did they forget? Or did they just learn to live with the discomfort?

I really want to understand. Because even though my hurts are *minuscule* by comparison, I still can't put them behind me. I haven't forgotten. I haven't learned to live with the discomfort. And as for forgiveness, then I have no idea what that means. What is this thing that people talk about so much?

It's now more than six months since my divorce was finalised. Over two years since Shaun and I separated. And life is good in so many ways. Yet still too many days are hijacked by resentment and anger. When I feel cast aside and worthless. When ugly feelings bubble up, accompanied by images of Shaun expecting me to fall into line with his agenda, speeding away as fast as possible, foot down hard on the gas as if I'm merely the opposition in one of his legal cases.

My resentment itches like crazy and all along, small acts of retaliation have brought satisfaction for brief, delicious moments. Short-lived relief like scratching an insect bite. Refusing to stick to his timescale. Standing up for myself in other ways. But in the long run they've achieved nothing. They've just added to the heat and anger. As Nelson Mandela said, 'Harbouring resentment is like drinking poison and then hoping it will kill your enemies.'

When will I be ready to forgive? Do I have to wait for some kind of apology? If so, then it's unlikely to happen.

And *how* do I do it? Do I have to tell Shaun that I forgive him? Would he take that as exoneration? Because I can't do that.

Be grateful for the good things. For my children…and the rest of my family…and Mike…and my friends…and my health…and sunny days…and birdsong…and flowers…and chocolate biscuits…and…and…and…

Think about those…

Change the way I feel…let go of the resentment and pain. Well…

…if I knew how to do that then I wouldn't hesitate. I'd do it right away.

Because I don't like feeling mean. I *want* to be a nice person. I *want* to feel good about myself. I really do. And I want to forgive because while I do not, I am spiky and unsteady. The thorns prick me. They make it difficult to trust Mike, and they hurt the children.

I'm a problem solver. Read up about it. Go for a walk. Have a think. Talk to friends. Make a list. Have another think.

There *must* be a solution to this.

18 Folgate Street

It's a drizzly evening, and I meet up with Emma outside Liverpool Street Station. We hug. She's just finished work and as instructed she's wearing pumps rather than her usual smart heels because I already know that we're going to be on our feet a lot. We dash along Bishopsgate, heads bowed against the rain and after zig-zagging all over the pavement to avoid the homebound City workers, it's a relief to turn into the relative peace of Folgate Street. Halfway along, we find what we've come for. Number 18 is an elegant Georgian townhouse with shutters on the lower windows, and a carriage lamp on the wall. It looks perfectly ordinary. There's nothing on the exterior to indicate that it contains what David Hockney has described as one of the world's five great experiences.

Tentatively, I knock at the door and immediately we hear the jangle of big old keys turning in a well-oiled lock. Inside, standing in the candlelit hallway is a woman. She nods. She's been expecting us. There's no small talk and once we're over the threshold and the door is carefully locked, she looks us up and down. She hesitates for a moment, appraising us to decide whether we are fit to proceed, and then she speaks slowly and clearly. 'Feel don't think. Look don't speak. Open yourself to the experience you are going to have.'

This is Dennis Severs' House where the rooms are set up like still-life paintings and as you walk through them silently, you experience the smells and sounds that a canvas can never provide. Its eponymous creator was a true eccentric – a Californian with an eye for drama who bought the house in 1979. It was in a derelict state and for the next twenty years, until his death, he devoted his life to restoring it.

We step into the kitchen. A couple of other silent visitors are already here and in the centre is a scrubbed pine table with a basket of eggs, a cut pomegranate with ruby seeds, and a phallic sugar loaf that makes me blush. Candlelight dances on the worn surface of the copper pans, and there are sweet tarts on the range. There is a delicious smell of spices and warm pastry, and on the table is a bowl with a partially-stirred pudding. It's as though someone was interrupted in their work and has stepped outside the room.

That's how it is throughout the house – you see signs of the people who live here, and you hear them but they're elusive. And that's because they're not real. The Jervis family – Huguenot silk weavers who bought the house in 1725 – are the product of Dennis Severs' imagination. As we wander from room to room and peer into the lives of generations of these imaginary residents, we step into still-life arrangements where everyday objects and half-eaten meals are left casually lying around.

Severs recorded sounds – of bottles being uncorked, glasses filled, fires poked and clocks wound – and these are played through speakers under the floorboards. He salvaged them from old televisions – the house might be elegantly decorated and stuffed with *objets d'art* but it was not a rich man's vanity project. He had little money and built up his huge collection of ornaments and artefacts by haggling with dealers and street market traders. Before he restored each room, he would sleep in it with just a candle, a bedroll and a chamber pot, exploring its personality. Then working late into the evening by candlelight, he arranged and decorated, using borrowed tools, timber from abandoned pallets, and the kerbstone outside as his sandpaper.

We go up the stairs and into the parlour which is a rich Regency green and smells of woodsmoke. There's a fashionable candied pineapple on the table – music tinkles, a clock chimes, the fire crackles, and we hear the sound of horses trotting past. The lady of the house has just popped out – leaving her earrings and fan on the side table, and weak tea in a bone-china cup. Severs wrote with longing about the importance of home and his search for its essence – perhaps because his mother died when he was eleven. He said it was not about possessions but about 'an atmosphere of safety in the love between my parents... in a tone of voice, in conversations... being busy in the garden.' This room is utterly peaceful and harmonious. I could stay here for hours.

Not so the dining room, which is a riot of male bawdiness with spilled drinks, overturned candles, upturned chairs, and a puddle of wax on the tablecloth. The revellers have just stepped outside.

Up another level, and in the main bedroom, a prickle of discomfort. I am a voyeur. This is where people are at their most exposed. The four-poster bed is rumpled and the dressing table is such a clutter of candles, feathers, and porcelain boxes, that there's too much to take in. Elsewhere in the room there's a dish of almond-stuffed dates, a water bowl on a stand, and a screen behind which I imagine Mrs Jervis might – just might – be undressing. We hear more horses trotting by.

A bell tolls, a dog barks, there are whispers, Mrs Jervis calls, and then we hear urgent footsteps. In a smaller bedroom there's a fire burning invitingly in the fireplace, and a side table with sewing, spectacles, and another half-drunk cup of tea. Under a wooden chair we spot a chamber pot and recoil at the sight of a yellow puddle. A glossy black cat sits on the bed with its eyes closed and paws tucked neatly out of sight. I mouth at Emma, 'Is it real?' She strokes it and nods. I follow suit and it bites me.

As we climb up through time to the top floor, we see the fortunes of the house transformed to a decaying slum. Here in the cramped attic resides what Severs called hopeless poverty – squalor, starvation, damp walls, overcrowding, disease, and despair. A meagre fire does little to relieve the bone chill and we hear the weak cry of a sickly baby. There are no rich Regency colours here. Instead, this chapter of the house's history is told in its cracked walls, dirty bed, and the poor-man's meal of oysters and cabbage on the table. Then we see a newspaper. It informs us that William IV has just died and as we stand here on the first day of Victoria's reign, we are time travellers. There's a frisson in knowing a little of what happens next.

Feel don't think

It's the end of our visit and as we step out of the final frame into the real world, we can at last break the silence. There's certainly plenty to talk about but the rain is lashing down as we dash back along Bishopsgate and it's impossible to say anything sensible. Then we spot a cosy pizza place, and have the same idea. We look at one another. And nod. Within moments, we've shaken off our wet coats and the server has us settled in a quiet corner.

Back and forth, we throw random ideas into the mix. We agree about many things that we have experienced this evening – the originality, the overwhelming number of objects, and the inscrutability of the cat. But we were struck by different things. I was stirred by the sounds – the clock, the horses' hooves, the whispers – and by the smells of baking and wood smoke. Emma was shocked by the temperatures – how the warm drawing room contrasted with the chill of the attic. And as we talk, I realise that we're searching for words that allow us to share our impressions but it was the *feelings* the experience aroused that made it special, and which are impossible to express adequately because they're so primitive – the essence of home, the desperation of poverty, and nostalgia for the past.

Then we get onto the stories that we couldn't resist concocting as we tried to make sense of it all. 'I think Mrs Jervis must have been having a problem with one of her servants,' I say. 'That's why she went off and left her tea.'

'No,' says Emma. 'A visitor had just arrived and she'd gone to check her hair was tidy.'

'OK then, what do you think about the dining room?' I ask.

'A row over gambling debts,' says Emma. 'It seemed bad-tempered.'

'Hmmm. Not sure about that,' I say. 'I think they were celebrating a business deal.'

Was Mrs Jervis getting changed behind the screen? We agree on that.

'She was getting ready for a ball,' I say.

'She was going to bed,' says Emma.

We're united about the baby's pitiful cries – heartrending. 'It was hungry,' I say.

'It had cholera,' says Emma.

It's fun speculating but the one thing we do know for certain is that we don't know. No-one really has any idea what was in Dennis Severs's mind. And that's easy to accept. Things get more complicated when there's emotional investment in the questions. Like wondering what was in Shaun's head when he decided our marriage was over. For many months, fragments of memories crashed around in my head as I sought answers. And as I did this, taming them into a story relieved some of the pressure.

He was on his raft with his story and I clambered onto mine with my story. And as we drifted apart there was less and less chance that we would ever understand one another. The law didn't help as the only way to get the quick divorce that Shaun wanted was for one of us to apportion blame to the other so he insisted that I cite his adultery, committed after we had separated. Maybe if we could have accepted that we just saw things differently, then we'd have got through it better. But as lawyers' letters flew around, we retreated to polarised positions where there was only room for one of us to be right or wrong, good or bad, cooperative or obstructive. Thankfully, the law changed in April 2022 and now one or both parties can apply for a no-fault divorce simply on the grounds that the marriage has broken down.

I still find myself drifting along on my raft, trying to understand what happened. Much less often than in the beginning but enough to send me off down annoying little creeks. But here's a new thought. Maybe I don't need a story anymore. Maybe I can decide to stop looking for any coherence because all I have is a confusion of clues and no story I concoct will provide a solution to the mystery.

I've come up with the phrase *resist the story*, and I'm going to keep it up my sleeve so I can pull it out like a handkerchief when I find myself in a creek. It pairs well with a Gallic shrug – the raised shoulders, upturned palms and wide eyes express the feeling so much better than the words *I don't know and probably never will*. I know that smiling releases hormones that make you feel happier and calmer so maybe a shrug does something similar.

I stow my shrug and *resist the story* phrase in my toolbox—grateful for this new equipment and an eccentric Californian.

Adapting

One of the biggest projects on my list is to watch *David Attenborough's Life Collection*. There are in total, seventy-nine episodes, spanning nine series and covering the animal and plant life of every kind of environment from deep oceans to jungles, and deserts to frozen tundra. Together, they provide an encyclopaedic account of the natural world and they are so brilliant that I can't fathom why I didn't watch them when they were initially aired – the first episode in 1978 and the final one in 2008. But then we all have gaps and my list is helping me to fill in some of mine.

Like my knitting project, this one stretches out over many months. I watch the episodes on my own, dipping in and out, and marvelling at the diversity and scale of the natural world. Who could fail to be impressed by the vital statistics of blue whales – their hearts are the size of a small family car and their testes weigh a ton. All genres are here – drama, tragedy, comedy, and creatures so strange that they could be extras in a science-fiction movie. There's also plenty of horror. One lunchtime I settle down to watch an episode from *Life in the Undergrowth*, and as I eat a toasted cheese and pickle sandwich, a Venezuelan centipede appears on screen, as big as David Attenborough's arm, and with the power of a small snake. It lives in bat caves and as I stop munching and watch with appalled fascination, it shins up the cave wall, strikes out at a nearby bat and injects venom from its fangs. Within an hour that bat's flesh is all gone.

Adaptation is at the heart of these programs and they show how exquisitely animals have evolved to suit different environments. I particularly like the frogs and toads. There are over five thousand species and they come in an incredible variety of colours, shapes and sizes. They've colonised every continent except Antarctica, and often have to face extraordinary problems in making a home. Evolution has overcome these challenges in ingenious ways. Sir David introduces us to a small plump creature that lives in Southern Africa, and in his trademark awed tones he tells us how this desert rain frog copes with the parched bush landscape by living underground. It digs itself a cavern and only goes above ground when it rains. Just a couple of times a year. Then there are the North American tailed frogs that make their home in fast-flowing mountain streams. Any other kind of tadpole would get rapidly swept away but these can anchor themselves to rocks using special suckers on their mouthparts. Best of all is the waxy monkey leaf frog. It is lime-green and lives in the treetops of Bolivia where it's hot and dry. It can tolerate an unusually wide range of temperatures thanks to a gland on its back which produces wax. Sir David is clearly captivated by the little creature as he watches it rubbing the wax all over its body, taking care to apply it thoroughly like a conscientious sunbather.

All of these creatures adapt to make a home. And now once again, so must I.

It's eighteen months since Mike and I had our first meeting – it was under the clock at Waterloo – and during that time as we've managed a long-distance relationship, I've come to know the hundred-mile drive that separates us, very well. But that is all about to change.

This will be my sixth home in nine years and I've come a long way from the first of these upheavals when Shaun and I had to sell what we had thought would be our forever family home. The one with the rare orchids in the fields, and the chickens and goats in the garden. During our time there we'd succeeded in filling it with happy childhood chaos but in doing so we'd stretched ourselves thin and we left ourselves financially exposed. Eventually, a few sharp slaps of bad luck toppled us into a position where we could no longer afford to stay there.

It didn't take long to find some enthusiastic buyers – a family of noisy Australians – and the day we moved to a rented house in a nearby town I consoled myself with the thought that there was more for teenagers to do there. They would spend less time being ferried around the countryside by car and could have some independence. After the removal men left, we shut our new front door on the boxes and experienced the novelty of being able to walk to a local restaurant. A trattoria run by a larger-than-life Sicilian who won seven-year-old Molly's heart by giving her samples of his home-made ice cream and telling her she was *bellissima*. There *were* compensations to losing our money. I could see them but for Shaun the loss of the home that he had been so proud to give his family, was a deep and complex grief.

Less than a year later, our hopes of being able to buy another house were dashed when he was made redundant and then within a few weeks came the worst blow of all. He had been unwell for many months with vague health problems that had impacted his ability to work but it was only when he collapsed and ended up in hospital, that we discovered the reason – he was suffering from chronic myeloid leukaemia. It was a dark and frightening time for us all. But a miracle gene-therapy drug got him back on track and then we were on the move again, cutting our outgoings and squashing into a first-floor flat. We settled in, and just over a year after moving, when it was starting to feel like home, the owners decided to sell. By this time Shaun had relapsed and his only hope was a stem cell transplant. He was confined to bed and while the hospital carried out a world-wide search for a donor, friends helped us move to our next rented home a few streets away.

We stayed in that house for eighteen months and during that time Shaun had his stem cell transplant – he discovered later that the donor lived in America and was of Russian heritage. There were many medical emergencies following that but eventually things began to look up in the realms of both health and work, and we were able to gather together enough money for a deposit on a modern house on a small estate. The owner had recently divorced and was selling up.

Now four years later that's me. I'd had hopes for this house. Maybe the previous owner had, too. But Shaun's heart wasn't in it. He went away at every opportunity, even leaving me to move in on my own. I told myself we were both working towards a new stability after all the turbulence. But *he* knew, *you* know, and *eventually* I did too, that it wasn't so.

I'm moving to Southampton. I've found a little terraced house just a mile away from where Mike lives, and Molly and I plan to live there until she goes to university. After that if all goes well, Mike and I will set up home together. It's too soon for the three of us to share a house – he has no day-to-day experience of teenagers and I want to enjoy Molly while I still have her. Things seem to be falling into place because even before this plan evolved, she had announced her intention to move schools after her GCSEs. Having spent five years at an all-girls school she is desperate to meet some boys – and fortuitously there is a large and excellent sixth-form college in Winchester, just a few miles from Southampton. When Molly and I go to an open evening she says that she loves it and wants to go there.

So here I am – in early September and surrounded by boxes. I've spent the past few weeks finding homes for things I don't expect to need in my new life. I'm ready to adapt to whatever comes next.

A new home

My sister comes to visit after the movers have gone. She's twelve years older than me and because of the age difference we've never had the kind of relationship where we kicked one another under the table or pulled one another's hair. Instead, she has been a role model. She found stability – marrying, supporting her husband in his career, making a comfortable home, and raising her children. When I thought about the kind of adult life I wanted, I looked to her. As a lawyer, Shaun had much better earning potential than I did and even though I'd had plenty of higher education, I valued a stable home life above everything else. It was easy to fall into traditional roles. Especially when we pursued the dream of a rural upbringing for the children. We couldn't both commute and so even though I worked on and off after the children came along, I thought of myself as a mother who happened to have a job, not a working woman with children.

My sister's life has turned out quite differently from mine. She has been married to the same man for forty-eight years and together they have four sons and twelve grandchildren. Now she's keen to see what this next phase of *my* life looks like.

Inside my new home, the echo of empty rooms is deadened by stacks of boxes. Mike's been helping all morning, excited that I will now be nearby and keen to make it as easy as possible for Molly and me to settle in. She's out at the moment, having her first day at sixth-form college.

I locate some mugs, instant coffee and chocolate digestives and go outside into the small garden with my sister, brother-in-law, and Mike. The previous owners have left a wooden table and some chairs on the paved area at the far end, and we sit there facing one another. I keep looking across the neat rectangular lawn towards the back of this red-brick terraced house – the first property I have ever bought on my own – and I am struck by all the things that have changed in the past few years. I raise my mug towards Mike and say 'My name is Lynn Farley-Rose, I live in Southampton, and this is my fella.'

My sister knows about me changing my name after being discarded but she's keen to clarify other matters. 'Why don't you call him your fiancé?' she says.

'Because he's not,' I reply, taken aback at her directness.

She turns towards Mike. 'Why don't you ask her?'

'Because I don't want him to,' I say panicking.

It's one of the few subjects that has been taboo between us. He was happily married and has grieved deeply for his late wife. I assume that he won't ever want to marry again. I'm not sure what I feel but I do know that I don't expect being with someone to be the solution to my happiness. Or theirs. I don't want to step into a wife-shaped space any more than I want Mike to fill a husband-shaped space. We have to make something new and different.

When Molly gets back she is pleased to see that the boxes and furniture from our old house have made it safely to this new house. She asks if we can go for a walk. That and sitting in the car are always our best times to talk. We walk along the local streets and over to the nearby sports facilities where girls with tabards are playing netball and runners are pounding round the athletics track.

'What if I don't like it?' she asks with a wobble in her voice.

Reader's block

It's mid-October. I made it my mission to get all the boxes unpacked as quickly as I could so as to minimise the uncomfortable liminal space between one house and another. And that's now more or less done. I work from home at my writing job and when the autumn sun is warm enough, I sit outside for lunch. If his teaching commitments allow, Mike comes to join me or I wander down to campus, buy a sandwich in the Student Union shop and join him in the university grounds, surreptitious with my magpie salutes. Sometimes we swim in the university pool.

The leaves are falling onto the patio at home and as I sweep them up our friendly neighbour leans over the fence and tells me about the succession of renters who have lived in the house. The previous owner didn't spend any more on it than he had to, but it is structurally sound and responds wonderfully to some loving care. I hang pictures, put down bright rugs, dot plants around, and paint the walls. Cool blue for my bedroom and lavender in the small square living room. It goes perfectly with the Victorian pine mantelpiece. Molly has got her room sorted to her satisfaction and already has a lot of coursework which she somehow manages to tackle in between parties and outings into town with her new friends. It's a treat to go in with her for late-night shopping, armed with a list of items that we need for the house. Browsing at John Lewis, deliberating, and grabbing some noodles at Wagamama.

I feel, tentatively, that day to day life is more stable than it has been for a long time, and with this I am hoping for the return of something precious that has mysteriously disappeared.

For over two years now, I have not been able to read.

I can, of course, understand the written word and for the majority of my life have carried a book with me. At all times. And a spare as insurance. But one of the casualties of marital breakdown has been my enjoyment of reading. It went into hibernation and lies out of reach as if buried under rotting leaves and damp moss. And it's not showing any signs of waking up. When friends ask about it I can only shrug my shoulders. Perhaps it is dead. Where once there was pleasure, inspiration, solace and escape, there's now a void. I think often of my mother's spelling problems and wonder if this is my version of what she had.

All along this has been perverse. Especially in the early stages when I would have most welcomed sanctuary from the jagged wreckage of everyday life. I tried again and again but the magic ingredient that converts the act of reading into something wondrous, lay tantalisingly out of reach. It didn't matter whether I chose fiction or non-fiction, my brain was an unmade jigsaw puzzle. If I was lucky, I might get the corners and some edge pieces in position. Then I could inch along and make a bit of progress. But I always got overwhelmed in the middle. Reading requires concentration and surrender. My mind by contrast has been restless, wandering away from the words on the page into past injustices and future insecurities. And it continues. Time after time, I read, re-read, sigh, re-read, and then discard the blameless book. Sometimes listlessly. Sometimes furiously.

Back in my old life, before I moved, friends invited me to join their book group and I accepted gratefully, touched at their efforts to cheer me up. And also hoping this would get me on the path to reading recovery. First up was Kingsley Amis's *Lucky Jim*. I started it… a few days passed…I started it again… This pattern went on until two hours before our meeting when I had no option but to speed-read the remaining nine-tenths. I sat on the bedroom floor warming my back against the radiator, and doing nothing more than getting through each page. Later, I had little to contribute to the discussion and hoped my friends would not regret having welcomed me into their intelligent and well-established group. A few months passed. More books. More joyless speed-reading. I always believed that books make the reader bigger. Broadening them out into new worlds and experiences but here I was, struggling to operate in my own self-contained world and I couldn't cope with extra stimulation. Eventually I made an excuse about work commitments and left.

This reader's block has also sabotaged my attempts to read all six of Jane Austen's novels. Saint Jane appears on my list because how can I join in any literary conversation if I have not read, and what is more, deeply appreciated all of her work? I am curious about it too as she has so many millions of devoted fans. As it happens, I'm pretty certain that I *did* read *Pride and Prejudice* in my twenties but it's hard to be sure as since then I've soaked up the wet-shirt TV adaptation and a memorable production at the Old Vic. It's the same with *Emma* – I know her well, even affectionately, but can't be sure where my memories and impressions have come from.

One thing is certain. Austen has captured a diverse range of hearts and minds in her butterfly net – women, men, academics, non-readers, feminists, misogynists, soldiers in the trenches, and literary giants like Scott, Tennyson and Kipling. Darwin read and re-read her novels and even Churchill is said to have turned to her for comfort during the Blitz.

This project was one of the first treats I began in the six months before Shaun and I separated, and I got off to a good start – *Sense and Sensibility, Pride and Prejudice*, and *Emma* were all enjoyable. I was glad to have read them. But then came the end of my marriage and the start of *Mansfield Park*. On the first attempt I managed thirty-five pages. Several months later I picked it up again and got through fifty-three pages. But since I'd had to re-read from the beginning this was a net advance of a mere eighteen pages. There was a third and a fourth attempt. I tried reading the words out loud, listening to an audio recording, and even moving a bookmark slowly down the page revealing one line at a time like an L-plate reader. All to no avail. Against my will, I remained uninterested, unmoved and unamused.

I ache to recapture the elusive pleasure of reading. Partly for its own sake but also because its absence is a reminder that I'm not fully healed from the divorce. I'm in a much happier frame of mind and am keen to move on but while this continues, I know that I am not yet whole.

2015

Simplify

The recent move was a new opportunity to prune my possessions and I welcome this process of contraction. It's the opposite of the relentless acquisition that was inevitable as our family grew and grew. Simplifying suits this stage of my life. I want to spend more time on relationships and doing things I value – less on caring for energy-draining clutter.

And it's not just about simplifying material things. Every family comes up with its own unique lifestyle recipe but it must be said that Shaun and I chose very complicated ingredients. After all, why send the children to local schools when you can have them at four different ones, requiring hours in the car with an impossible schedule so you're always late for someone? Why live within your means when you can be mortgaged to your limit and constantly uneasy about money? Why have a manageable garden when you can have a huge one that requires you to spend half the weekend mowing it? And in Shaun's case why spend hours each week commuting to a job in London that sets insuperable targets and makes you constantly stressed? The answer to these baffling questions, and many more, is that we started out young, energetic and healthy – we thought we were invincible and that things would only get better. What we didn't know was that job loss, financial catastrophe and cancer were louring in the background, hands in pockets like bad guys waiting for their moment – wise to the fact that when people stretch themselves thin, something has to give.

There's nothing wrong with striving for a good life – we wanted our children to have a better upbringing than we'd had ourselves. But expansion was hard to resist. Way past the point when we had enough to make us happy. It masqueraded as progress and once we were on that treadmill then acquisitions gave the false assurance that we were in control. Success is seductive and it's hard not to compare yourself with friends and neighbours, especially when you live in an affluent commuter village where the bar is raised. Massively. If all around you people are having swimming pools installed then you wonder if you're out of step by not having one. It's disturbingly easy to lose touch with reality.

It's a relief to have emerged from the rabbit hole where I believed that complicated is inevitably better. When I was dealing with the tangled bureaucracy that accompanies a divorce, I wrote myself a note and pinned it above my desk. *Don't make problems where there aren't problems* was a mantra that pulled me back from frustrated tears, many times. And the more I relax into simplicity, the more useful the idea becomes. It pops up in unexpected places. Most recently in my fish project.

I love fish and would happily eat it every day. But although I enjoy cooking, this is an area where I lack confidence. There's a lot to contend with – bones, sandpaper scales, bendy fins, reptilian skin, and sad little faces. These all make its preparation quite intimidating. Not to mention the fierce recipe book warnings about overcooking. These make me nervous – they imply that a minute too long and my efforts will be wasted.

I would like to overcome these barriers and so my list includes a fish-related item. I want to cook ten different varieties and to end up with a recipe for each that I deem a success.

When I tell Molly about my fish ambitions, she looks impressed. 'Are you going to catch it yourself?' she asks. And as it turns out, the sourcing of basic ingredients is not as easy as I anticipate. There are times during this project when I wonder whether her suggestion might be easier.

I decide to start with plaice. Something familiar and therefore not too daunting. A peruse through my cookery books leads to the plan of stuffing it and I set off to the supermarket with my list. Prawns, garlic, two lemons, a bunch of flat-leaf parsley and two whole plaice. But as a fresh-fish-buying virgin I didn't bargain on the fact that late on a Monday afternoon, two whole plaice are hard to find. I wander around disconsolately and that evening we have pasta.

I abandon the plaice plan and the following week I turn my attention to skate. I've had this with black butter in restaurants, and like it very much. I identify a promising recipe and once again I need lemon and parsley, as well as capers, butter, white wine vinegar and two skate wings. I've got an hour for lunch so I set off in the car with my shopping basket. At a large branch of Sainsbury's I tick off nearly everything on my list and then join the queue at the fish counter. The fishmonger looks professional in his white coat and boater and I place all my confidence in him. But I'm misguided.

'No' he says. 'We don't stock skate. Try Asda.'

I'm still learning to navigate around my new city but know enough to be aware that Asda is a fifteen-minute drive, and my lunch hour is rapidly disappearing. I thank him, swear politely under my breath and pay for the fish-related items in my basket.

Back in the car and on my way to Asda, I salute a single magpie and then spot a branch of Waitrose. I'm sure they can be trusted so I pull into the car park. 'Do you have a fish counter?' I ask an assistant, ever so slightly urgently. She smiles reassuringly and points towards the back of the store. There, I find a beautiful array of fish, all pink, white and grey with the odd bit of parsley scattered about. And to my relief I count six skate wings lying there enticingly. There are four people in the queue ahead of me so I resolve to wait patiently and try not to worry about the fact that I've already used half of my lunch hour. Salmon for the first customer. Cod for the second. Scallops and monkfish for the third. And five skate wings for the fourth. Yes. *Five* skate wings.

I've rarely disliked anyone as much as this customer, and glower at her as the assistant packs the fish into a bag and hands them over. Then it's my turn. 'I need two skate wings,' I say looking sadly at the singleton on the slab. 'Do you have any more?' The young assistant goes off to check. She's only gone for three minutes but this is a significant proportion of my remaining lunch hour. No luck. I toy with the idea of sharing one wing between two of us, but that seems a waste of effort so I do a bit more swearing under my breath and set off for Asda.

Another fish counter that looks inviting. And I count four skate wings. There are three people in the queue so I fidget and glare suspiciously as each one is served. Smoked haddock, prawns and cod are dispensed efficiently and then it's my turn. 'Two skate wings' I pant, waiting for the hitch. But there's none and the assistant pops them into a bag, and then seals and weighs it. She attempts some pleasant conversation but I grab the bag and dash to a vacant checkout. I put it on the conveyor belt and once again am faced with a chatty assistant. As I get my purse out to pay for my one item, she smiles.

'That *was* a nice easy shop,' she says.

That evening, I chop and stir and as if by magic, the kitchen fills with evocative beachy steam. It reminds me of Devon pubs. Fortunately, after all that effort, the skate with black butter is delicious.

The next Monday it's seared scallops with a light dressing made of garlic, olive oil, finely chopped vine tomatoes and herbes de Provence. Rick Stein's recipe doesn't disappoint. And nor does Asda. I get what I want straightaway and even have time for a lunch-hour sandwich. Things in the world of fish are looking up. I'm pleased to report that the monkfish and tuna experiments are successful, too and all the recipes are at the end of the book.

By the fifth fish, I notice a change in my attitude. The path that has seemed strewn with hazards, is starting to feel smoother. It's nothing to be scared of. It's just a piece of fish. Bake it, grill it, fry it. Maybe a bit of simple sauce... I don't even bother to follow a recipe when it comes to lemon sole but instead cut it into fingers, dip these in beaten egg and breadcrumbs and fry them for a few minutes. We have them with sweet potato chips. We were also going to have peas, but I accidentally tip them down the sink, so we have a hastily assembled watercress salad instead. It is all extremely good.

Fish number six – sea bream – marks the start of some freeform experimentation. I am definitely feeling more confident and the fish itself is a revelation. Firm in texture and with a delicate flavour. An added bonus is that it's very cheap compared with some of the other fish I've bought recently. I brush the fillets with a mixture of curry paste and yogurt and while they're grilling, I prepare a simple bed of tinned green lentils, chopped beetroot, thyme and walnuts. It's all remarkably easy and quick.

Hake is number seven and by now I've grown in confidence so much that I've ditched the cookery books. It's a firm fish and well-suited to a Mediterranean treatment so I spread it with a little red pesto, parcel it up in foil and bake it in the oven. While it's cooking, I sweat slices of red, orange and yellow peppers in olive oil spiked with a little paprika. These make a soft, pleasantly fleshy base on which to place the fish and I serve it with spinach and a contrastingly crunchy *very garlicky garlic bread*. The leftover peppers make a delicious cold salad for lunch the next day.

Swordfish comes in steaks a bit like tuna and can apparently lack flavour so I marinate it in some chilli-infused olive oil which also prevents it from drying out. I serve it with some mushroom rice to which I add a handful of chopped wild garlic foraged from Mike's garden. It smells like a Spring country walk.

Sticking with the theme of quick and easy, the Thai sea bass with rice noodles turns out to be one of my favourites. Coconut milk with tiny broccoli florets and thin sticks of carrot, flavoured with green curry paste and fish sauce, garnished with finely chopped salted peanuts and some basil.

I'm pleased to have so many new dishes in my repertoire. As soon as I realised that home-cooked fish can be delicious without fancy sauces and reductions then keeping things simple has worked just fine. The notion of simplicity seems to go against that of growth. To learn how to be simpler seems counterintuitive but it *is* what I've done.

That's nine different kinds of fish. One more to go.

Riding on branch lines

I'm sure that herring, sardines and pilchards *can* be delicious but as I'm not keen on small bones they haven't made it onto my shopping list. I need to find a different species for my tenth and final fishy flourish.

I've exhausted all the likely options at the Asda fish counter so I'm going to have to look further afield. My best bet is the fish stall in nearby Winchester market, and if I'm going there then I may as well take a day off and enjoy my outing. It's a reminder that the point of the list is not to tick things off but to have some fun and enjoy new experiences.

Another advantage of going to Winchester is that while I'm there I can visit the antique clock shop in the city centre as I need some advice about an oak mantel clock which once belonged to Shaun's grandmother. I've lavished money and attention on it over the years but it's never worked properly and now I'm giving it one last chance.

I wake up early and feel terrifically happy when I remember that it's a treat day and I can do exactly what I want. I love that I have no idea how it will turn out – which unexpected branch lines it will send me along and what will have happened by the end of it. My favourite example of a day turning out unexpectedly is the man who got a surprise when he checked his PayPal statement. The company had accidentally credited his account with the entire

PayPal economy and he had a balance of 92 quadrillion dollars. Not every day can be that good – though PayPal did rapidly correct their mistake – but I'm starting out optimistically with this one.

I arrive early at the market with my clock in a plastic carrier bag and am delighted to see an enticing display of fish, many of which I now recognise. I hesitate over the huss but eventually opt for turbot. They are large so I ask the fishmonger to select the smallest one, and he weighs it and wraps it carefully in paper. It's significantly more expensive than any of the other fish I've bought during my project so I hope it's good. The neighbouring vegetable stall is selling some tempting new season asparagus so I get a bunch of that too.

Across the road I spot a fabric shop and am reminded of a problem that's been bugging me ever since I moved. My bedroom overlooks the neighbour's garden and while she's hanging out her washing and I'm getting dressed, we regularly surprise one another. Although I've managed to avoid net curtains for most of my life, I decided recently that I must now yield to modesty. The shop has an impressive variety of patterned nets but none of them appeal so I buy two metres of plain muslin.

By now, I'm a bit weighed down. The fish is heavy and the bags are banging against my legs. The clock clangs as I walk and every now and again it makes a half-hearted attempt at a chime. Then, as I make my discordant progress through the city centre, I notice Winchester Cathedral and it occurs to me that I could soak up a bit of history before going home. A couple of minutes later I am at the main door and as I step inside, the clock chimes five o'clock which is both embarrassing and inaccurate.

'I'd love to look around,' I say to the man at the ticket desk, 'but I've got a lot to carry. Could you possibly look after this?'

I hand him my clock and as I do so it makes its preparatory whirring noise and attempts to strike again. 'Could you take this, too?' I add handing him a large flat parcel.

'What is it?' he asks suspiciously.

'A turbot,' I reply.

'A what?'

'A turbot. Oh, and I've got this,' I say, handing him the muslin curtain.

I pay for my ticket and the assistant is directing me towards the guided tour when he notices that I have a bunch of asparagus sticking out of my bag. 'I suppose you want to leave that too,' he says.

The next hour is absorbing. I stand on Jane Austen's final resting place in the nave and squint up at the window that's dedicated to her memory. My fellow tourists coo and purr at the mention of her name. And I keep quiet about my struggles with *Mansfield Park*. At the top of the window is a pane depicting St Augustine from whose name, Austen is derived. I tread over thirteenth-century decorative floor tiles, and as I turn a corner towards the high altar my jaw drops at the enormous, ornate stone screen.

Another highlight is the story of the hero who saved the cathedral from collapse. Because the foundations were so weak – essentially a wooden raft on top of a peat bog – there had been a great deal of subsidence and flooding over the centuries and pumping out the water only made the subsidence worse. So, in 1905 William Walker was brought in. He had trained as a Royal Navy diver and over the course of the next five and a half years he worked steadily, spending half an hour every morning getting into his diving suit and then plunging into the water under the cathedral from where he would pull out peat with his bare hands, then replace it with bricks and concrete. His work was done in complete darkness and he would emerge after his three-hour morning shift to smoke his pipe and eat a mutton pie before starting the afternoon session. By the time the task was completed, he had used 25,800 bags of concrete, 114,900 concrete blocks, and 900,000 bricks. And he clearly did an excellent job as the cathedral has moved no more than a millimetre in the past century.

At the end of the tour, I return to the desk. I'm looking forward to coffee and a brownie in the cafe next door. 'Please could I have my clock, asparagus, muslin curtain and turbot?' I say. The obliging attendant looks relieved to see the back of me and my bags, and I am pleased to have spoken a sentence that I've almost certainly never said before. In fact, I have to wonder whether anyone in the history of the English language has ever spoken that particular combination of words. If they have, I'd certainly be interested to know what they were doing.

Back home, in the evening I struggle to fillet the turbot and wish I'd asked the fishmonger to do it. Then I roast it with a little garlic and a splash of white wine. We start with the lovely bendy asparagus spears – too young to be woody, and delicious with black pepper and butter. The fish was so expensive that it needs to be the main act, so I serve it with a simple accompaniment of spinach and mashed sweet potato. The flesh is juicy, firm and pure white, and it tastes of the sea. It's a sensory treat.

The verdict on the clock, incidentally, was that it's not worth the cost of repair. But notwithstanding the death throes of the clock, I had a surprisingly joyous day out. And like I said – it's not *just* about the ticks.

Where did you park?

I have to meet up with Shaun as Molly wants us both to attend her sixth-form parents' evening. It's been several years since we've seen one another and I can't deny that I'm dreading it as all the old feelings of hurt, anger, and confusion rear up.

For several days before the meeting, I feel unsettled and anxious. I fidget and go for walks in an effort to stay calm. There seem to be more magpies around than usual and whenever I spot one, I make sure to do a deliberate and unmissable salute.

And yet as so often in life, the anticipation turns out to be worse than the reality. When I'm faced with the solid actuality of the man with whom I shared my life for so many years, these feelings turn out to be bluster. They slink away and instead I feel numb. We sit side-by-side on plastic school chairs as our daughter's teachers discuss her progress with us. We listen, nod and ask a few questions. It's all straightforward, and Shaun takes careful, lawyerly notes. At the end we both stand up and he turns towards me. He is going to say something. I wish he wouldn't. My heart jumps and I brace myself for a fresh wave of pain.

He looks unsure of himself and gives a tentative smile. 'Where did you park?' he asks.

'A couple of streets away,' I reply.

There's a silence. I feel I should ask something about him in return. But I don't want to risk causing damage to this fragile civility. Then I have a flash of inspiration.

'And where did *you* park?'

'Down the hill,' he replies.

'Oh,' I say, 'Nice.' And then as we can't think of anything to add, we go our separate ways.

In the days that follow, I think about the strangeness of this encounter and remember how in the months after the break-up I grasped at any straw that might offer answers to the unanswerable questions – When will I feel normal again? And in my darker moments, *Will* I feel normal again?

I floundered about amongst feelings of anger, sadness and denial but the more stable state of acceptance seemed mythical and unattainable. I feared that I would fall apart and could not fully believe that I would ever get to a place where I was not internally protesting and fighting the changes that had been foisted on me. But in the light of my parking chit-chat with Shaun, I see that at last something has shifted. During that exchange, I may not have been able to summon up sparkling conversation but I was no longer bursting with questions about why he wanted to end our marriage, and why he saw things so differently from me.

It has taken several years to realise that the answers to these questions, once so feverishly sought, will never be found. They are buried deep. I imagine them under piles of leaf mould, disintegrating and rotting so that if either of us even knew where to look, they would have been transformed beyond any kind of truth. Above them, is a weight of earth that has accumulated over time, and they are tethered by tiny tenacious roots and thorny weeds. The painful and painstaking effort of digging deep to unearth and disentangle them would be to no avail. They are in the past and I no longer need them.

I think at last I might have grasped something of what acceptance is. I expect there will be setbacks, but overall, it feels like progress. It may even be a step towards forgiveness.

Fifty-two films

Henry has been living in Paris as part of his studies but now he's back in the UK and comes home for a week of reading and revision. It's good to spend time with him and everything seems to be going well until one morning when I'm in the kitchen planning what to cook for dinner and he comes in looking uneasy.

'Mum… is everything alright?'

'Yes, of course,' I reply.

Rather briskly as I'm weighing up the relative merits of lasagne and onion tart. 'Everything's absolutely fine. Why?'

'Well…I couldn't help noticing the list you'd written on the kitchen blackboard. It says *Clean bathroom – Hung out washing – Buy anti-snoring device – Get fence mended – Murder!*'

By the latter part of the week, I've worked my way through all those things and have a new list. *Take parcels to Post Office – Cancel dentist – Ring Barbara – Buy vitamin tablets – Blackmail.* It's another ordinary week in suburbia.

It's also the week in which I finish my Alfred Hitchcock project. A couple of his early silent films are lost but fifty-two are available on DVD, and as a compulsive completionist it's no good watching some, I've had to watch them all. It's taken quite a few months – *Murder!* and *Blackmail* are the final two.

I've already revealed my enthusiasm for classic films with my Billy Wilder treat, and Hitchcock was another obvious candidate for my list because he created so many powerful images that have infiltrated popular culture. I may have been on my own as I did a section of the North Downs Way, but he was with me in spirit. As I plodded along the edge of a ploughed field, I noticed a tractor going up and down in the distance. Up and down. Up and down. It was dry with a light breeze and everything felt still. Quiet and rather sinister. A small plane circled in the sky above. Round and round. Dipping and diving. Apparently aimless. Was I imagining it or were there more birds than usual? They were settling on the telegraph wires…

And I've never forgotten a landlady I met in Cambridge about twenty years ago. Shaun and I had to go to a function at his old college and we stayed nearby in a small terraced house. The owner lived there with her elderly mother and ran it as a B&B. Our room was simple with a few dust-free ornaments, faded floral wallpaper and turquoise nylon sheets that refused to lie flat. The next morning, we sat with several other guests in the front room making desultory conversation while our hostess trotted in and out with plates of egg and bacon, humming to herself. Later as we stood in the narrow hall waiting to settle our bill, I read a newspaper article that had been cut out and pinned to the noticeboard. It reported how a burglar had broken into a terraced house in Cambridge in broad daylight, terrifying the lady owner and her disabled mother. 'That's us,' said our hostess proudly as if drawing our attention to a glowing review. And she started to hum again.

I haven't watched the films in any particular order. There has been much to enjoy, even in those I already knew. It may have been the fourth time I'd seen *Psycho* but I was almost taken in by Norman Bates who seems such a pleasant, puppyish young man. Janet Leigh's heavily pencilled eyebrows, the motel, and the spiky score all combined to make me feel thrillingly grubby. Other pleasures have been new. I particularly enjoyed *Sabotage* with its prewar London cosiness and a discordant moment that left me reeling. Even Hitchcock thought he'd gone too far.

Shadow of a Doubt was another satisfying discovery – a strong story and reputed to be Hitchcock's own favourite. I was surprised how much I liked *The Manxman*, a powerful silent film about a love triangle, and although the plot of *North by Northwest* is ridiculous it's always a joy to watch Cary Grant who remains handsome, polite and wryly amused throughout his many tribulations. His grey suit is immaculate from start to finish and was voted the best suit in film history by a panel of fashion experts.

There's pleasure in the completeness – it means I can pick out a favourite and for that I'm tempted to choose *The Wrong Man*. It's the only one based on a true story and Henry Fonda is marvellously dazed as a decent man who is wrongly convicted of armed robbery. But in the end, it does have to be *Vertigo*. This was the third time I'd seen it, and even though I was no longer startled by the plot twists, there was much enjoyment to be had in admiring how Hitchcock manipulates his audience. For days afterwards I was haunted by the hallucinatory title sequence and Bernard Herrmann's romantic, urgent score which installed itself as an earworm.

As I watched, I noticed more and more of this idiosyncratic director's themes. He used birds as a marker of impending doom long before the terrifying intensity of *The Birds*. And he was fascinated by trains, recognising the dramatic opportunities offered by narrow corridors, secluded compartments, slide-up windows, social intermingling, dark tunnels, and menacing whistles. Margaret Lockwood and Dame May Whitty are wonderful in *The Lady Vanishes* but the true star of the film is the steam train which puffs its way through prewar Europe while the plot unfolds on board. Another of his directorial quirks comes from his love of dogs. If one of his characters owns a dog you can be pretty confident that they are of sound character.

Blondes are one of his most well-known obsessions and he almost certainly had crushes on a number of his female leads. In spite of that, he was devoted to his wife Alma Reville who worked on many of his films as a screenwriter and editor and they were married for fifty-three years. But it wasn't a conventional marriage and there has been much speculation that he was terrified of sex. He joked that it happened just once in order to conceive his daughter and even that was done with help from a fountain pen.

He was never awarded an Oscar despite being nominated five times. But perhaps that reveals more about the Academy and what motivates its voters' decisions. When they did *finally* give him a Lifetime Achievement award in 1968, he went up to the stage to receive it and as the audience waited for a sparkling acceptance speech, he made his point with an expressionless 'Thank you' and a long plod back to his seat.

Now that I've reached the end of my Hitchcock marathon I'm pleased to have engaged with *Murder!* and *Blackmail* but I've also discovered that not all of his output was good. I should have known to expect that and it was no different with Billy Wilder. There was brilliance but there was also mediocrity and some films that I didn't enjoy at all – *Jamaica Inn, Secret Agent,*

The Paradine Case, Under Capricorn, Juno and the Paycock, the strange musical *Waltzes from Vienna*, and his final film *Family Plot*. Even Hitchcock admitted that he disliked some of his films.

I got myself thoroughly hung up on completionism but there's a niggling feeling surrounding all of this. It's pushing me to challenge yet another mindset that's been in place for decades. Did I really need to watch them all?

The Fifth Battle of Mansfield Park

I'm still not managing to read for pleasure and my pile of discarded books continues to grow along with my frustration. Then one day, unexpectedly, I have a breakthrough. I'm chatting with a friend who has also been through a divorce and much to my surprise she tells me that in the aftermath she too, could not summon up the concentration to read. It went on like that for about five years and then as silently as it had disappeared her enjoyment came back. Until this moment, I've not heard of anyone else having this problem and imagined I would be stuck, forever chasing an old pleasure that refuses to be captured. But my friend's experience gives me cause for optimism. Perhaps it is just a matter of time and so I should stop fretting about it.

I clear my bedside table and where there was once a reproachful pile of books there is just a glass of water.

For the first few days I'm delighted to have more space both next to the bed and in my head. But there's a contrariness to desire and removing the pressure makes something shift. Those empty spaces feel *too* empty. And so, within a week of adopting my indifference to fiction, I find myself having an illicit scan of my bookshelves and am moved to pick up an old favourite – *The Light Years*. It's the first volume of Elizabeth Jane Howard's *Cazalet Chronicles* and just a couple of chapters in, I know that

I have found my literary Eden – a large, comfortable house in prewar Sussex where I reacquaint myself with the cast of characters I loved when I first read these wonderful books twenty years ago. Over the course of a month, I devour all five volumes and when I reach the end, I am bereft. I'm in stellar company as Hilary Mantel called Elizabeth Jane Howard's novels exquisite and said there is no author that she has recommended more often to her writing students.

EJH wrote with great insight about relationships, perhaps because her own personal life was so turbulent. She had many affairs and Kingsley Amis was her third husband. His writing was taken seriously while hers was frequently relegated to the cupboard labelled *Writing by Women for Women*. 'I always played second violin to him,' she said in a radio interview and I do enjoy the irony of knowing that she succeeded in rescuing me from my reader's block while her husband with his self-consciously clever *Lucky Jim*, failed so dismally.

Buoyed by the joy of reading fiction once more, I'm ready to re-engage with some unfinished business – *Mansfield Park*. Some critics have drawn parallels between Jane Austen's writing and that of Elizabeth Jane Howard. They both write elegantly and weave skilful plots but their subject matter is low key, dealing mostly with the minutiae of people's lives rather than the grander, shoutier matters of power, politics and warfare. Another similarity is that they set their stories amongst the upper middle classes. This could make them narrow but they are written with such intelligence, humour and subtlety that they have a wide appeal. And as Hilary Mantel observed, both writers are less cosy than they appear – beneath Austen's sprigged muslins and EJH's convivial dining tables, there is an edge.

Conveniently stranded in bed with a chest infection I prepare for the fifth Battle of Mansfield Park. I'm braced for defeat but this time there is no struggle. I make it through to the end and then reach for my dusty copies of *Northanger Abbey* and *Persuasion*. I read, cough, read, snooze, and read some more. And then suddenly they are done. I have now read all six novels. To my great surprise given the battles, I decide in the end that I like *Mansfield Park* best of all. Fanny Price is a perplexing and frustrating heroine, and the plot is not at all predictable. *Emma* comes in at number two. She's a very different kind of heroine, infuriating in her conviction that she always knows best but so well-meaning that I'm willing to overlook her failings.

Now that I've read all of Austen's novels, I'm curious to know more about her life so I dip into a couple of biographies – and there is no shortage to choose from. I read how at the age of twenty-five she was unhappy to be uprooted from her childhood home in the Hampshire village of Steventon when her father made a sudden decision to retire from his post as rector and move the family to Bath. She had been writing but following this upheaval she seemed to stop for quite a few years. The biographer Claire Tomalin argues that having so little control over her situation may have triggered a depression and brought back memories of earlier traumas such as being sent to boarding school, and being dangerously ill with typhus at the age of seven. Other biographers interpret the gap in her writing differently but this interpretation rings true to me. When faced with turbulent emotions, I couldn't read and she couldn't write.

Four years into his retirement her father died and from then on as an unmarried woman she was at the financial mercy of male relatives. Fortunately, her brother Edward was wealthy and offered a cottage on his estate where she could live with her mother, sister Cassandra, and a family friend. They settled happily in the village of Chawton and it's probably no coincidence that with this new security she returned to her writing in earnest. It was from this cottage that she wrote so contentedly to her brother Francis that 'When complete, it will all other houses beat.'

This house is now open to the public and as it's only twenty miles from Southampton, I decide to round off this particular treat with a morning out, seeing the place where she wrote the majority of her novels. The drive through Hampshire countryside is thoroughly enjoyable with its sweeping fields stretched out golden in the sunshine, and I love the feeling of connection to this, my new home county. When I get to Chawton, the museum turns out to be an intimate cottage and I spend an interesting couple of hours delving around in the relics of her life and watching a short film. In one of the rooms, I stand next to her small, round writing table and read that in her day, the nearby door had a useful creak, granting time to hide her manuscript whenever anyone approached.

Afterwards, at the village cafe named in honour of Cassandra, I sit outside with a warming bowl of vegetable chilli, and then I linger with my hands cupped around a large coffee. It's a still moment in an otherwise busy week. I like to think of Jane writing in this village with stagecoaches trotting past her window, carrying passengers to London, Portsmouth, Newbury and Bath.

I, too, am happily settled in my home and it comes with several favourite places where I settle down and read. But I have to say I'm not likely to be found with a Georgian novel on my lap. I admire her writing but I'm not sucked in by Austenmania. My preference is for characters with a more modern outlook that I can really relate to. Less constrained and restrained. I am, however, much more warmly disposed to her than DH Lawrence who called her 'thoroughly unpleasant, English in the bad, mean snobbish sense of the word.' Mark Twain also put the knife in. 'Jane is entirely impossible. It seems a great pity to me that they allowed her to die a natural death. Every time I read *Pride and Prejudice,* I want to dig her up and hit her over the head with her own shinbone!'

I have to question why he kept reading *Pride and Prejudice* if he disliked it so much but leaving that quibble aside, it's all further evidence that even when you try to do your best you can't please everyone. It's just the way it is.

Awkward questions

If you've been following carefully then you'll know that since the start of this book, I've finished four complete sets of creative output – twenty-six films directed by Billy Wilder, fifty-two by Alfred Hitchcock, seventy-nine episodes of David Attenborough's Life Collection, and most recently, all six of Jane Austen's novels. And *complete sets* is the key phrase here. That's important. Because this chapter is all about completeness.

I was proud of myself for completing these sets. It showed commitment. That I am not a Mr Toad figure who gets all the kit and then flits from one enthusiasm to the next. And I enjoyed crossing off each completed item on its sub-list, and then crossing off each completed set on my master treats list. I love using my pink highlighter pen. But… I have to admit that it's not *all* rosy. If I'm going to be honest with myself – and that *is* a relationship I am trying to cultivate – then I'm feeling uneasy.

There are, of course, things that have to be finished. But this book is not about work and duty. It's about treats. And the treats themselves have prompted me to recognise that I suffer from compulsive completionism. It's another of those mindsets that I acquired early in life and which has wrapped itself around me like a spider's web. This one binds me to the belief that I've started so I must finish. Regardless of whether I need to do it or am finding it interesting.

At this point I ought to say that if you do not have a completionist mindset then my contortions may seem odd. Even crazy. But before dismissing them with a shake of the head and saying 'Well just don't do it then,' spare a thought because there are almost certainly people in your life who do think like this. I can think of several family members and friends who do.

Shining a bright light on this mindset gives *it* nowhere to hide and *me* a lot to think about. But it's bossed me about for a long time and isn't ready to give up without a fight. First up for the defence is the observation that those seventy-eight films, seventy-nine TV programmes, and six novels were there to be enjoyed.

Unfortunately, that is not entirely true as I found some of them positively tedious. I ploughed through them and allowed finishing to puff itself up into an accomplishment. But when challenged, it quickly crumples and I see it for what it is – a ridiculous habit masquerading as an achievement. It's not even as though anyone cares except for me. I get sucked in by the Sunk Costs Fallacy which whispers mischievously that I've already invested some time in whatever it is, so it's best to continue. Not true. A smarter choice is to cut my losses at a half-watched film or partially-digested book and move on to something I prefer. Another mischievous whisper tries to tell me that *maybe* if I watch or read right to the end then I'll find that this tiresome offering is really rather wonderful. Occasionally that's true. But mostly it's not.

Another argument put up by the defence is that by completing each set I will be more informed and therefore an all-round better person. If only that was as straightforward as it sounds but the bald truth is disconcerting. I remember lots about a few of them, random snatches from others and then there's a miserable little bunch that have left no lasting impression. Beyond the stand-out exceptions, I can't even be confident about which I liked and disliked. I'm unreliable. I watched some of the films while I was feeling alert and enthusiastic but others got an unlucky slot where I nodded off or was distracted. *Mansfield Park* repeatedly got short shrift and then when I was in the right frame of mind I enjoyed it. Even *Vertigo* which I admire so much now, left me unimpressed when I first saw it some years ago. This is all unsettling and makes me feel yet again that I don't know who I am or what I feel.

Finishing is like a toddler demanding that you do what it wants. And so long as you hang on in to the end it will shut up. But there's an older sibling who is also part of the completeness family, and this one is complex and needy. *Thoroughness* requires careful handling or you get sucked into its neurotic shenanigans and it asks awkward questions about whether your life is worthless without it. Here's an example…

I'm feeling content because I've crossed lots of items off my list and pacified the Finishing toddler. But then Thoroughness pops up and murmurs slyly in my ear. 'You know all those films that you only watched once. Well wouldn't you have got more out of them if you'd watched them again? Remember what happened with *Vertigo*?' And Thoroughness has a point. My viewing was incomplete even though I'd finished the films. But how many times would I have to watch them for it to be thorough? Would it only be when I'd noticed every detail? Is the experience worthless for being incomplete?

And then, just sticking with Hitchcock, there's the irritating observation that my list of his work was not complete. These were just the films he directed. But he also directed seventeen episodes of the TV show *Alfred Hitchcock Presents*, as well as presenting over three hundred more. Should I include these, and maybe those from his early days in the film industry where he was an assistant director or title designer? Clearly, I've just exaggerated myself into silly territory but here's the thing – the biggest problem with completeness is that it can never be satisfied because even though it snaps at me, it doesn't really exist. Like the wind, it blows me about but there's nothing to grasp.

'Why should any of this matter?' I can hear you say. 'It's just about books, films and TV programmes.' But the reason it matters is that this mindset is insidious and has spun its web around my attitudes to other things. Like work, where despite training and qualifications I've rarely felt that I know enough to be competent, let alone expert. Instead of making the best of what I *do* know, it's the missing bits that chip away at my confidence. Maybe with the external validation of one more course, one more test then I will know enough, I tell myself. Maybe then I will know everything in the same way that the first encyclopaedia compilers aimed to gather together the sum total of human knowledge. And I know I'm not alone. Imposter Syndrome – the feeling that you're not worthy of your position and will eventually be revealed as a fraud – is commonplace.

These mindsets need a kick. They're bending me out of shape and I've let them get away with it for far too long. And so this is where I intend to part company with complete oeuvres and to make *Incompleteness* my friend. If I'm wondering whether to give up on something I'm not enjoying I've told this new companion to ask me two questions –

Do I need to do this?

Do I want to do this?

Sometimes I might request more time to make my mind up. But if the answer to either question is *yes* then I'll carry on with it. If the answer to both is *no* then I won't. Instead, I'll give myself a pat on the back and do something more worthwhile. And if I start to slip into old habits then my new friend will remind me that I no longer need to fear missing out on something wonderful. They will explain patiently that this is because it's better to be *happy* about the things I am doing rather than *unhappy* about those I am not.

Trapped

'I never knew who she was,' says my sister. 'I didn't understand her. And she didn't understand me.' I nod. We often muse about our mother. Much less about our father. He was absent so much. And when he *was* there, he didn't say much.

It was 1943 when our parents met at a dance hall in London. She was twenty-four and by her own account, not very worldly. He was five years older, raised in the East End and a good dancer with a resemblance to Clark Gable.

That's pretty much all I have to pick over. Bare bones. Neither of them reminisced about a romantic courtship because there was no love story. He said nothing at all about what happened next so what little I know came from her. She discovered that she was pregnant. There was a hasty hushed-up marriage. And then there was her father's disappointment. He disapproved of my father but as a successful publican he helped them get the tenancy of a pub that they could run together in North London. His disapproval grew as he saw my mother working hard to build up the business, and my father drinking too much.

They had a family by then. My brother was born six months after they married, and my sister two years later. But eventually after several years everything fell apart and my mother took the children to live in a caravan with her. She found a job in a bus garage and was rebuilding her life when my father got in touch again. He had moved to Dartmouth and was working at the naval college in his original trade as a welder. 'Come and join me,' he said. 'Let's try again.'

'He promised it would be better this time,' she used to tell me. 'He promised we'd buy a house. But we ended up *here*,' she'd cry, pointing in despair at the damp bathroom and the mouldy windows where condensation froze on the inside. 'A *council* house.'

By then she was well and truly ensnared. And I was the biggest trap of all, arriving uninvited a few years after the move, and twelve years after my sister. My father wasn't made for family life and when I was two, he announced that he was off in search of work elsewhere. Because he could. My mother was back on her own, trapped by poverty, and by Dartmouth itself – a small, beautiful town forced into remoteness by miles of twisty country lanes in one direction and a river in the other.

'I really *am* going to learn to drive,' my mother would say, her eyes shining with dreams of escape. But she believed she was trapped and so it never happened.

My brother escaped as soon as he could and my sister looked after me while my mother worked in a bar. Then when I was seven my sister did the sensible thing – she married and moved away.

From then on, I was trapped too. I believed I would eventually escape but until that day came, I was stuck with just my mother. Six evenings a week, she took me with her to the seedy hotel where she worked. 'You've got to be good or I'll lose my job,' she'd say. 'They only let me bring you as a special favour.' So, I stayed out of the way in a top bunk in one of the tiny bedrooms while she served drinks and made tinkly conversation in the bar downstairs. I listened to the radio and read until I fell asleep. When the bar closed, she'd come upstairs and slip into the bottom bunk.

One night something different happened. There had been a ball at the Naval College and unknown to me, she went there for drinks after work. I dozed and when the bedroom door opened, I sat up expecting to see my mother. Instead, a man lurched into the room and I'd spent enough time hanging around the bar to recognise that he was drunk. He was *very* drunk. He looked at me vacantly and nodded, and I, brought up to be polite, nodded back as if we were two adults passing one another in the park. Then he swayed to the sink and as he did a lot of noisy vomiting I sunk down in my bunk and became invisible. When he was empty, he fell onto the bottom bunk and immediately began to snore. I waited until I could be absolutely sure he was asleep and then crept down the ladder. I opened the door slowly and silently and wandered the corridors until Margy, one of the young bar staff found me. Much as I tried to make it look perfectly normal for an eight-year-old to be wandering around alone in her nightie late at night, she knew it wasn't and kept me safe in her room until morning. My mother never acknowledged my terror. 'Oh, I know who *he* is,' she said about the intruder. 'He wouldn't have hurt you.'

It happened again. A different drunk this time. He was much older and came in through the window. I've blotted out what happened but I do know I wasn't physically harmed, and I learned that I couldn't trust my mother to keep me safe.

I wonder now how she could have let that happen. And how she could dismiss it so easily. She got more upset when she mislaid her glasses. Or worst of all, the diamond ring her father had given her. A reminder that she had once been loved. She never found that love again. *My* father broke her nose, gave her a great scar down her left cheek and got three months in prison. Many years later when I'd grown up and left home and my father had died, she married a widower named Douglas. She was full of hope but it didn't work out. They fell out about whose daughter's photograph should have pride of place on top of the television, and about morning radio stations. He wanted Radio 2 and she favoured Radio 4. The final bust-up came when his daughter served swede with the Christmas turkey…

My mother longed for her life to be different. She felt she had little control over anything. Money. Love. Health. She never trusted her body and expected it to let her down at any moment.

She passed on some of her fears collection to me. They snuck in and took up residence so that my twenties were constrained by panic attacks, and phobias of vomiting and degenerative disease – unhappy feelings that feed on a dread of being alone and vulnerable. They still lurk like monsters in the understairs cupboard and I try not to prod them. There are many reasons to keep saluting the magpies.

2016

Fear of painting

I want to produce a piece of art that I can frame and put on the wall. It's something I've never done and I like the idea of pushing my boundaries and creating something I can look at with pride.

While it stays on my list unaddressed, then all possibilities remain. It's a vague mission and that suits me as I need time to let the idea mature. But something's wrong. Instead of looking forward to it, my misgivings are growing like weeds.

The problem is that too late, I'm having to face the hurdle of not being able to draw. 'Oh, we're not artistic in this family,' my mother decreed from as early as I can remember. 'We're hopeless. When I was at school, I was so bad at art that the teacher got me to sit in a big hat and the other children drew me.' I absorbed this unquestioningly. What she believed about herself must be true for me, too, because she said it was. It was the same with sewing and sport.

I don't remember much about art at secondary school. Only that I didn't feel it was aimed at me and I dropped it at the first opportunity.

My belief that I couldn't draw was consolidated by my terrible handwriting – in itself an exercise in reproducing recognisable shapes. I can usually read my own writing but don't always have such luck when other people are involved. If I had to go out, I would sometimes leave my teenage children a note asking them to do a few small jobs. More than once I got back and was greeted crossly. 'We spent ten minutes looking at the note you left and none of us could read it.' This always ended with a triumphant, 'So whatever it was you wanted us to do, we *haven't* done it.'

As groundwork for my art treat, I do some reading about drawing. It's true that some lucky people are blessed with a particularly good visual memory. This makes it easier to remember the relationship between lines and angles and to transfer them to the page authentically. But I'm encouraged by research carried out at University College, London which suggests anyone can learn to draw. The problem lies in *believing* I can't draw. Most people don't practise enough and like me, many are put off at an early stage when they're told that their attempts don't look like they're supposed to.

Despite discovering this, I'm still wary of trying to produce anything representational and continue to mull it over. Eventually, I settle on a vague plan for an abstract painting – like a patchwork quilt. I'll have to think carefully about the patterns and colours and maybe I can incorporate a few meaningful words, too. It will require care but at least I won't need to draw.

I could do this on my own but it's beginning to feel too much like an exercise in getting-it-done. This isn't what I wanted at all and I know it will be a richer experience if I get some expert guidance. Then, as with the crossword treat, I realise that I know someone who might be able to help. Claire is an old friend of Mike's and a talented portrait artist. She's warm and one of the things I value most is that she's never afraid to disagree. 'I like that because...' I might say quite innocently, and she will often come back, 'I *don't* like that because...' We often agree to disagree but she always makes me think. When I ask if she could help with my project she agrees at once. As a relatively new friend, I hadn't realised that she used to be an art teacher and has a special interest in helping people who don't think they can draw or paint. I'm thrilled and a bit terrified.

I explain about my crippling lack of artistic confidence and my ideas for an abstract piece. 'Hmm,' she says. 'I work by getting people to think of vivid childhood memories. When they try to capture them on paper, they forget their inhibitions.'

'But I don't *want* to draw,' I say.

'Have a look at some Chagall paintings,' is her response. 'He put all sorts of motifs in his paintings. Things that he remembered from his childhood and which were significant to him.'

She gives me a smart black notebook, and we set a date for a few weeks hence when I will go and spend time at her home studio in Leicester. In the meantime, I have instructions to think about childhood memories and to gather some relevant images from books and the internet. There are things that are seared into my memory and others that I haven't thought of for years.

On the agreed day I have an early breakfast and am in Leicester for mid-morning coffee and a planning chat. I show Claire the ideas that I've captured in my notebook and then we go through to the studio which is full of light and overlooks the garden. She hands me a blank canvas. Twenty-four inches by twenty inches of stretched white space. Maybe I could just leave it as it is, and put it in a fancy frame – call it *Canvas 0.01* or something inscrutable like that. I share my nervy joke with Claire. She looks brisk and shows me how to mount the canvas on the easel.

Within a few minutes I'm making tentative pencil marks. It's hard not to view it as *spoiling the canvas* but I work on creating the central section of this memory painting about the town where I grew up. I want it to show the River Dart with houses rising up the hill. The river gives the town its character and purpose – fishing, sailing, ferries, boatbuilding, smart seafood restaurants, the Annual Royal Regatta, and the Britannia Royal Naval College where generations of naval cadets have messed about in boats. I recall how there was always a faint smell of seaweed in the ancient streets.

I've gathered some pictures of the town and Claire reminds me to look closely and to copy what I see. I sketch in a band of river, with houses above, and then bands of meadow and sky. My marks look childish but the thing that amazes me is that they *are* recognisable as houses. After lunch we talk about paint colours and how to mix the right shade on the palette. Claire gives me a paintbrush and I start filling in the shapes. Sapphire blue for the river with shady banks in navy blue. Yellow and pale brown for the houses with dark brown roofs and tall chimneys. The windows are black-rimmed squares. I'm enjoying this. Then I make a smudge. 'Don't worry,' says my teacher. I dab my brush over the smudge and it disappears. The grass is Spring green with yellow flecks of flowers.

From the age of eleven I crossed the river every day by ferry and then took a steam train to school. After the original line was shut down it was restored as a heritage railway, and as the local grammar school was next to Churston station, we were allowed to travel on it. For a few months in the summer of 1973, it was the Flying Scotsman. The train *has* to be in my painting. It represents my journey to education and that enabled my escape.

I copy an image and focus on drawing the individual lines and angles rather than the whole thing which is overwhelming. I can't depict the sulphurous coal smell, the smuts, or the sunburned tourists but they're all part of the memory.

The next day I start on the motifs that will form side borders. I draw a stick child. I thicken her legs with wellies, and clothe her thin body with shorts and a t-shirt. I put a straight stick in her crudely depicted hand and add a triangle at the end. That's a fishing net. She stands within her own little panel in the border, and I paint a cloudy blue sky behind her head. Her boots turn red, her hair brown, her shirt orange with three decorative black buttons above her denim shorts. That's me. I've been sent out to play on the Embankment while my mother is doing a daytime shift in the bar. I'm slipping about on the seaweedy steps leading down to the river, all ready to catch tiddlers in my stiff little nylon net.

About half of the canvas is covered now. And that's the end of my first painting experience. Claire says that it's charming. She will let it dry and then store it carefully in her studio. We agree to fix another time, some weeks ahead, for me to go back and complete it. I drive home and wish I could feel proud of what I've produced.

Why do I find it so hard? Claire did everything she could to make it a happy creative experience so the problem lies firmly with me. I haven't yet been able to challenge that message that our family is not artistic. And there's another more damaging message that I swallowed whole. You must judge yourself accurately. If you do not do this then people will laugh at you. But worse than laughing to your face, they will laugh behind your back. So, if you dare to stick your neck out and try something for which you have little experience and no innate ability then you will be forever haunted by fears of being thought ridiculous and of putting yourself above your station. My parents didn't talk to one another often, but they did enjoy sharing a bit of casual mockery. 'She thinks she makes good pastry. That pie…' sniggered my father about some unfortunate amateur baker he came across. 'It was like a bit of old cardboard.' I can only imagine what he might have thought of the naive painting I have been working on today.

I don't believe that my parents meant to be cruel but they *were* judgemental and dismissive. Surely, all these decades later, I can escape these inner voices. Surely I can enjoy the process and not worry about the end product. But the truth is that I'm finding it astonishingly hard to take any pleasure in what I've produced.

I deal with my art project in the easiest way – I try to forget about it. And while I would not wish fire or other disaster to befall Claire's house, I do hope that my artwork gets lost. Maybe her cleaning lady will think it is rubbish and throw it out.

The end of a walk

I've loved walking the North Downs Way. When I made my list over four years ago, I chose it over other long-distance trails because all the stages from Farnham to Dover were accessible as day trips. But that was when I was married to Shaun and expected to stay that way. That was when I lived in Kent and had no plans to move.

I did half of the total distance and then there was a hiatus while I absorbed the shock of separation. When I picked myself up and started again, I was raw and terrified by three fierce dogs and a large drop of rain on my shoulder. Solitude was just what I needed at that time but since then I've walked other stretches in good company. Mike joined me on a sunny day for the section from Harrietsham to Charing, passing cornfields and large houses as well as a marker stone informing me that I had now walked 92 miles from Farnham. It had taken a long time. And a lot had happened.

Since moving to Hampshire, it's been more difficult but my kind, quirky friend Rachel prodded me to continue and kept me company from Boughton Lees to Etchinghill. I decided to miss out the optional loop that takes in Canterbury and now I am nearing the end of the trail. There is just one section left and that will take me to the chalky white cliffs and big skies of Dover.

The excuses of the winter come and go and then I get an image in my head of walking through flower-strewn fields with Henry as the English Channel comes into sight. He says he is happy to join me on this concluding stage but finding a date we can both do is the first hurdle, and we postpone several times.

When the agreed day finally comes, we set off from home at 7:30am and with dire traffic it's midday before we get to our starting point in the village of Etchinghill. It's all felt like quite an effort but I know this is something I want to complete. Those two questions are easily answered. Do I need to do it? *No*. But do I want to do it? *Definitely*. The walking itself has been marvellous and I love being able to look back and see the trail as a continuous thread through times of change.

Later, as I sit high on a headland with Henry, the late-Spring sunshine scatters diamonds on the sea. The white cliffs of Dover are still some distance to our left and the noisy transport hub of Folkestone is on our right. We eat roasted sweet potato and salad sandwiches made from Henry's homemade bread, drink lukewarm coffee, and chat easily. There's an exciting moment when we look down from the cliffs and see a train snaking into the earth at the start of the Channel Tunnel. It's strangely thrilling to think that when it emerges it will be in a different country.

It's a strenuous walk today with lots of steep ups and downs and by the time we are on Shakespeare Cliff with a grand view over Dover harbour, my feet and knees are all protesting. The great medieval fortress of Dover Castle looks down over the town – it vies with Windsor for the title of largest castle in England. From the cliffs it takes a surprisingly long time to descend into the town and when we get there, I am determined to seek out the official end of the walk, even though I'm hobbling by now. We meander round the town centre past a number of boarded-up shops and eventually find it on the seafront. Embedded in the pavement is a simple strip of black granite with the word FINISH facing the water, and START facing the other way.

Once I've seen that, I'm ready to set off for home. But first we need to get back to the car and in order to reach Etchinghill we have to take a train to Folkestone and then a bus.

'When's the next train to Folkestone?' I ask the ticket clerk at the station. 'September,' she replies and smiles. I give an automatic smile in return and then remember that it's currently May. We hadn't heard that the line got swept away in the Christmas storms. So we get a couple of buses instead.

The journey in the car is quicker than it was this morning and I'm grateful for Henry's quiet support and his company. It's increasingly rare now that he's a busy young adult with his own life. We talk and then he closes his eyes for a well-earned rest. As I drive along the M25 and the M3 towards home I think back over the sections of this trail and the impressions that are stamped in my memory – dappled woodlands, quiet lanes, steep climbs, streams, brick viaducts, Neolithic burial chambers, sheep, thatched cottages, ugly developments, bulls, quarries, vineyards, fly tipping, primroses, bluebells, barns, chapels, wallflowers, greenfinches, the noise of the Medway Bridge traffic, cake, being sad, being cashless, being elated…

It has been a multi-layered experience and a true treat.

Dutch courage

One of the benefits of having a treats list has been receiving relevant presents and last Christmas I was given two guides to The Netherlands. I'm planning to spend a week there soon but this treat is different from other recent travels. Its defining feature is that I will be travelling alone. Some years ago, I took Will to Stansted Airport and as I waved him off, aged twenty-three with a rucksack on his back and no fixed plans beyond a flight to Prague, I had a wave of regret that I'd never travelled with such freedom. No-one in my circle took a gap year and later came a long period when holidays centred round a troop of small children. I remembered this feeling of regret when I was making my list and decided it was not too late to have my own independent adventure.

By the time I get round to this particular treat it's still about having fun but it's also about something else. My life has changed considerably, and with Mike I'm keen to avoid past pitfalls. I've picked up enough relationship jargon to know that what I want is interdependence – being close but without compromising who we are. The trap to avoid is co-dependence, one of us denying our own needs and relying on the other to provide self-worth and purpose. I'm not sure how to get it right but Mike worries much less about this. He has the benefit of a successful marriage behind him. All

I have is the knowledge that my marriage went wrong and in its dying days a friend told me that I started to disappear. The focus had been on Shaun and his illness for so long that I no longer felt I had the right to want anything for myself. Liberation came unexpectedly and was uninvited, but I know for sure that I must not risk losing this liberty. I cannot allow myself to disappear again.

On Good Friday morning, I drive Mike to Gosport Marina and drop him and his huge kitbag on the jetty. He's delighted to be doing a week's sailing course. I go back home and pack my rucksack with the bare minimum of clothes and quite a few books, then I heave it on my back and set off along suburban streets. It takes an hour to reach the airport. I could have taken a taxi but walking there symbolises the freedom I hope to explore this week. I'm off on my Dutch adventure.

I've chosen this because The Netherlands is easy to get to, and has many places I would like to see. I was tempted by the bird-filled wetlands of the West Frisian Islands, and the Hanseatic League trading towns of Overijssel but in the end I settled on Delft for half the week and the port of Enkhuizen for the rest. Both offer plenty of opportunity for local exploration and for going further afield if the fancy takes me.

Several hours later I'm checking into my Airbnb in Delft. The room is simple and my host is charming. He recommends a family-run Indonesian café next to one of the many canals in the city. It's just what I need. The staff are friendly but demand nothing of me, and the food is cheap and comforting. The salt, lime and chilli perk up my taste buds and I eat slowly through a plate of spicy smoked mackerel, kale in coconut milk, and peanut noodles while wondering what to do tomorrow.

My normal approach would be to plan things out in advance. To have a structure and keep busy. But here I want to be spontaneous and see how that feels. When you plan, it compromises your freedom to some extent. When you don't, you're forced to confront the emptiness.

Next morning I decide that what I would most like is to take a train and gaze out at the countryside. So, I set off for Utrecht. My guide book tells me that it's hipsterish and has the biggest student population in the country. The canalside bars are packed in the Spring sunshine and I need some lunch so I queue at a street stall. It may only be a crusty white roll filled with tuna, onion, lettuce and tomato but it's called a *broodje tonijn* and that automatically makes it more interesting. I sit on some steps above the canal and watch the boats passing by.

Later, I leave the city centre and walk along peaceful streets and canals until I reach an extraordinary, flat-roofed white building with various thin vertical and horizontal structures in primary blue, red and yellow. This is the Rietveld Schröderhuis, a UNESCO World Heritage site. It's a Mondrian painting in 3-D and a unique example of De Stijl architecture. I know that Mike would find it as pleasing as I do and I study the details so I can tell him about it. But that won't be until I get home as we've agreed not to phone one another. An important part of this trip is to know I can manage on my own. And I've told my adult offspring that they can contact me in case of emergency but not for advice about how to remove a splinter, how to deal with mould on walls, or how to complete their tax return.

Two days later I take the train north to Enkhuizen. The journey is a couple of hours but I never mind spending time on trains. They're good companions, like locals dashing around showing off their country to me. I sit on the top deck and marvel at the breathtaking free spectacle of the tulip fields – broad stripes of red, yellow, purple, cream, orange, and palest pink, stretching towards the horizon.

My accommodation for the next few days is a sailing ship. It's more than a hundred years old and has been beautifully restored. Sandra, the owner takes groups out in it but she's in harbour this week so it's just a *base* for me. It's surprisingly comfortable with central heating, showers, five cabins, a galley, and a mess room with a big table. The overwhelming impression is of glossy wood and I'm glad not to be staying in a bland hotel. It turns out that I'm the only guest at the moment and I have a cabin with a narrow bunk and a washbasin. What it lacks in space it makes up for in atmosphere. There's even a ship's cat – a little tabby. I give her a stroke and then she jumps off the ship and scampers away to explore the harbour.

I sleep well, and the next morning Sandra produces a magnificent breakfast with a selection of bread and pastries, cheeses, fruit, yogurt and fresh coffee. We eat together and she tells me about shipboard life and her childhood in communist East Germany. Her independent lifestyle and single-handed ability to manage a ship makes my adventure seem embarrassingly slight. But I also know that there's no need to compare – everyone needs to find their own level. She asks what I'm planning to do today and on a whim, I say that I'm going to Edam.

It takes an hour by train and bus, and when I get there, the town is absurdly pretty with canals, gabled houses, cobbles and bicycles. But it knows that it's charming and the streets are lined with opportunities to remember it through the eponymous cheese and other souvenirs. I have a coffee at a pavement cafe and then hop on a couple of buses and cross a causeway to the small island of Marken in the Markermeer lake. It's atmospheric with wooden houses on stilts, old fishing nets, a picturesque lighthouse and views of the lake with dinghies scudding along in the breeze. But by mid-afternoon, I'm on my way back to Enkhuizen. And I'm still restless so I get off the train at Hoorn. I wander round the harbour then stop for a coconut sorbet. This fills some time. Now what? It's Easter Monday and everyone but me is in a couple or family group.

Being in the midst of jolly Bank Holiday people and yet apart, highlights the difference between solitude and loneliness. One so welcome, the other not. 'Pull yourself together,' I think sternly reminding myself that this is both self-imposed and temporary but the fact is that while loneliness is defined as an absence it is also a presence and so it's hard to ignore. And it's familiar, going all the way back to long evenings alone in a hotel room as my mother worked in the bar downstairs. I do all I can to avoid those memories mostly by keeping busy but today they seep in like gas. I can smell them and feel the clown with the sad mouth sitting on my shoulder.

There is only one option and that's to befriend myself. And as I'm feeling hungry, I look for somewhere to eat. The obvious choice would be a fast-food place where I can be invisible, but I pass a smart restaurant and before I know it, I'm inside asking for a table. I haven't brushed my hair all day and am wearing scruffy trainers and my old red cagoule with its mysterious black stains. Fortunately, the lights are dim. Various large plants interrupt the lines of vision, and there are buddhas and a fountain. The menu lists an eclectic selection of Asian-influenced dishes and the atmosphere is quietly respectful suggesting that food is taken seriously here. Feeling vulnerable brings heightened sensitivity to the slightest of slights but my waiter is exceptional. He makes me feel that I am as special as any other customer, recommending choices and inclining his head solicitously. There are long, positive pauses between the courses and I eat and drink slowly, savouring every moment. There is blackened cod, sashimi, a tiny rich chocolate pudding with exotic fruits, and a pot of jasmine tea. Everything looks exquisite and by the time I leave, my spirits are restored.

Next morning I share another breakfast with Sandra. I tell her about my crazy day of rushing around but I can't tell her that I was lonely. We all cover our tracks and avoid giving off the faintest whiff of it. Perhaps living on her boat with strangers coming and going, she gets lonely, too. As I step off the ship her little cat chirrups and stops for a stroke.

I head back to Delft for two nights and on my final day I go to Rotterdam. It's the largest seaport in Europe but it's the modern architecture that has drawn me here. The Centraal railway station plays an overture to the city with a swooping asymmetric stainless-steel roof and it's where I begin my self-guided architectural walk. Some critics describe Rotterdam as soulless but I enjoy wandering amongst the strange angles and experimental shapes. Mike would love it and notice different things from me.

This week I've proved to myself I can be self-reliant but it's time to go home. Will I do this again and if so, will I meticulously plan ahead? Or will I confront the emptiness? The answer is that I'm already wondering about a week on my own in Denmark—and I've no idea what I'll do when I get there.

Ruts

I never saw any evidence that my parents reflected on their problems. In particular, their relationship and how they might improve things – they just drove backwards and forwards along the same rut like a car bogged down in mud.

'It's all about the talking,' says Mike. So we talk a lot.

It's a revelation to share my 'fears collection'. I've not let it into the light before. But little by little, I let the bottled-up demons leak out. And I attempt to explain. Always expecting that he will find them incomprehensible and want to run a mile. But he doesn't. He listens and is interested. Kind.

He's so right. It *is* all about the talking.

Things change

One of the challenges in navigating a list is knowing when to deviate from it. In theory, as it's my game and I'm the only player, then I can do whatever I want. But time after time I come up against something that runs deep – my need to *stick to rules* – and this gets in the way.

Fortunately, there aren't many rules to this game – after all it *is* supposed to be fun, but one guiding principle is that once made, the list stays as it is. If I chop and change, I fear that I will regress back to earlier, hectic times when I felt like a small tree trying to put down roots on shifting sands.

Conceiving a list is simple. But as I found with the jacket and the painting, some treats don't develop in a straightforward manner. At times I have had to adjust my expectations and remind myself that they are not tokens in a ticking-off exercise but are instead experiences to explore.

Stay at the Burgh Island Hotel is proving to be one of the more problematic treats. It's an Art Deco hotel on a private 26-acre island opposite Bigbury-on-Sea beach in Devon. When the tide is out, you can walk there but for much of the day the sands are submerged and then the only way to reach the island is in a sea tractor – a curious vehicle that churns through the waves on giant wheels while the driver and passengers sit on a high platform. Agatha Christie stayed there several times and it provided the inspiration for *And Then There Were None* about a group of guests staying on a small island and being murdered one by one.

A beautiful hotel…a romantic island…a quirky means of transport…fabulous views... What's not to like? The problem comes when I try to book. I want to go with Mike and I also want to take Emma and her boyfriend Matt with us because of all the people who are dear to me, I think she will get the most out of it. She has her own treats list and it includes reading all of Agatha's novels. To make it worth our while we'd need to spend two nights there, and while the price is probably not unreasonable for such a special location there is no way round the fact that £2000 is considerably more than I can justify – especially for such a short stay.

So, Burgh Island Hotel sits there on my list as I wonder what to do. And then I have a brainwave. Maybe we could stay nearby and just go for Sunday lunch.

An efficient, friendly receptionist confirms that we can book lunch as non-residents and explains that on the day of our visit, we will need to call from Bigbury Golf Club, which is the last reliable mobile reception before the beach car park. The tide will be out at that time and so the hotel driver will bring the Land Rover over to collect us. I take a deep breath and amend the wording on my list to *Visit the Burgh Island Hotel*. The treat is saved.

Before our visit I read up on the island's history. Some time around 1400 it's believed to have been bought by the de Burgh family who also owned the Isle of Wight. But it came into its own in the Roaring Twenties when Archie Nettlefold commissioned a large, white, country house in the fashionable Art Deco style.

He was a socialite who dabbled in the financing of films, plays and expeditions and was a grandson of one of the founders of Guest, Keen and Nettlefolds, now known universally as the engineering giant GKN, but famous then for manufacturing nuts, bolts and screws. A weekend at his Devon retreat was *the* invitation for the Bright Young Things. Noel Coward went for three days and enjoyed himself so much that he stayed three weeks. Today's hotel rooms recall many famous visitors from the age of speed, jazz and luxury travel including Nancy Cunard, Malcolm Campbell, Amy Johnson, WO Bentley, and Josephine Baker. The Fruity Metcalfe suite is named in honour of Major Edward Dudley 'Fruity' Metcalfe who accompanied Edward, Prince of Wales, as an aide on his travels including frequent trips to Burgh Island. Then of course, there is the Christie Room and an Agatha Christie beach house as well as rooms named in honour of Hercule Poirot and Jane Marple.

The building has been through many changes. It moved from being a private retreat to a hotel in the 1930s but just a few years later was severely damaged by wartime bombing. In 1948 it was restored under new ownership but fashions changed and by the sixties it had been converted into self-catering holiday apartments. When Tony Porter and his wife bought it in the eighties it was in a sorry state. They had made a lot of money from founding London Fashion Week and they sank most of it into returning the hotel to its former elegance. Within a few years of its relaunch in 1988, it was named by Vogue as the best hotel location in the UK.

Our trip comes round quickly and we collect Emma and Matt from Totnes station on a hot day and take them back to our AirBnB cottage which is about ten miles away, at the end of a long farm track. As we bump cautiously along the ruts of red Devon earth, a couple of pheasants dart across in front of us, flapping and shrieking. We shopped on our way down and I enjoy familiarising myself with the small but well-equipped kitchen, recreating a delicious fennel and lemon risotto that a friend made recently, and a rich mousse especially for chocolate-loving Matt. We sit in the tiny courtyard garden till late, catching up on news.

The following day we dress carefully for lunch – jackets and ties for Mike and Matt, and smart summery dresses for Emma and me. She has her trademark *unbelievably high heels* and big sunglasses. We drive down miles of narrow lanes and at Bigbury Golf Club we ring as instructed to alert the hotel that we're on our way. The receptionist tells us to wait in the beach car park and to look out for our driver who is setting off as we speak. The beach is crowded and as everyone around us is wearing next to nothing, I am conscious of looking inexplicably formal. Fortunately, the driver is waiting and whisks us off across the sand. The hotel is a sleek white liner with metal windows in peppermint green. And we are film stars.

The green and white gates glide open and a receptionist takes us to the Palm Court Lounge for pre-lunch drinks. My jaw drops. It is *beautiful* – all gleaming brass and glass, small round tables, Lloyd Loom chairs and polished wood, with upright flower displays and palms providing height. We sip on cocktails where Churchill, Eisenhower and Wallis Simpson have sat before us and gaze up at the stunning stained-glass dome inspired by a peacock's tail.

I spare a moment to be grateful. My greatest fear about the divorce was that our family would disintegrate. The future was no longer what I thought it would be. I had a fixed image of the children coming back as adults to visit their father and me as we pottered around in our retired years. I was absolutely rigid for a long time in not wanting the divorce. It felt like the worst possible thing that could happen. It was a step into the unknown and it was scary. But here we are now gathered together in a changed formation that is a new kind of normal.

We chat quietly, all on our best behaviour and then a waiter ushers us into the restaurant where our table is waiting, next to a window with huge views over the sea. Almost all the ingredients on the menu have an asterisk next to them signifying that they are from local suppliers. I start with grilled Brixham mackerel accompanied by poached rhubarb and fennel ceviche. Mike has heritage striped tomatoes with a Manchego panna cotta. The mackerel is perfect and to follow I have teriyaki salmon, Asian mushrooms and crunchy green vegetables. I finish with red berry sorbet while Matt purrs over his chocolate pudding.

After coffee, Emma heads off to reception. Ever observant, she spotted earlier that there's a croquet lawn and so we collect a couple of mallets and four balls and she takes off her shoes. It's a lot of fun and I finish last. A ship's figurehead leans forward into the garden as if trying to listen in on guests' conversations and we round off our visit with a stroll around the island. It would only take fifteen minutes if you walked briskly but we meander along taking in the unusual features that make the most of being by the sea. The Mermaid Pool is a natural seawater lagoon surrounded by rugged rocks. There's a rowing boat in the middle and a wooden diving platform. The gulls scream and the waves break against the cliffs. There are no dolphins today but they are frequently spotted in the bay during May and October. It's hard to imagine a lovelier place.

We stop for a quick drink at the fourteenth-century Pilchard Inn. It's open to the public and has a couple of small rooms with low ceilings and bare stone walls. Then it's time to go back to the real world. The tide has gone out and so we get to travel on the sea tractor. It's certainly an unusual form of transport. The platform has a roof and open sides with horizontal rails that make it look like a large packing crate. Anyone can ride in it for £2 but today we are guests of the hotel. Over the years various ideas were proposed for how to get visitors across the water – a cable car, an underground train, and landing craft called Terrapins. But the sea tractor won out and this model was designed by a hydraulic engineer in 1968 in exchange for a crate of champagne.

Burgh Island has been through plenty of changes like we all have to. In the words of the Buddhist nun Pema Chödrön, *Things come together and they fall apart. Then they come together again and they fall apart again.* A cycle of order and chaos – that's just the way it is.

Two poems

We were in a coffee shop in Johannesburg and I was toying with a croissant when Mike turned to me with an anguished look. We were on holiday back in his old country, celebrating his sixtieth birthday. 'I want you to marry me,' he said out of the blue. 'I was going to ask you in the game park next week but I can't wait till then.'

'But surely you weren't surprised,' said friends when I told them.

'I was,' I said. And I really was. He was happily married before and I thought he wouldn't want to do it again. So I had put it out of my mind.

He *was* happily married before. And so was *I* – for many years until everything changed with illness and all the other things that went wrong. So perhaps it's not surprising that we both like being married. Going to sleep together, waking up and building shared routines.

We agree that this time round we want to keep things low-key and wonder about going off on our own to a Scottish beach or a Caribbean island. But we quickly realise that what we want is a celebration with our closest family and so that's what we do. We are fourteen in total.

I wear a long strapless white dress. A proper wedding dress but not a meringue. I'm not planning to ever marry again so I may as well enjoy it. I've got flowers in my hair and our local florist has made me a bouquet of exquisite pink peonies.

Emma and Molly are bridesmaids in matching short flowery dresses. They look beautiful, and my four adult children lead me into the registry office. Mike is waiting in a grey linen suit and open-necked pale pink shirt. He looks beautiful too, and very tall. One of the things I like best about him is that he has deep laughter lines around his eyes. But right now, he looks serious.

'Who gives this woman to be married to this man?' says the registrar.

'We do!' shout the children in unison and I hear a small sob in the congregation.

The registry office is set up for live streaming and I see Mike's sister and two brothers peering into their screens in South Africa and Australia. Instead of choosing a reading we decided to each write a poem. It's my turn first. Mike keeps my gaze as I read it. 'Top *that*,' says the registrar turning to him. He reads his poem and at the end she smiles, puts her head on one side, and nods.

My mother is there in spirit. I know she wishes me well. She reminded me earlier about the something old, something new, something borrowed and something blue. And she will be relieved that neither of us dropped our wedding ring. That would not have been a good omen.

After the ceremony there are photos in the old courtyard. Then we walk through the streets to the Indian restaurant where we had our first date in this city that is now our home. It's a Tuesday lunchtime and they're opening just for us. My high heels are pinching my toes and it's raining but neither of us can stop smiling. 'Marry someone cheerful' is amongst the wisest advice I ever heard.

It's quite simple really. We appreciate one another. We both lost what was precious and we survived it. Now it's up to us to make something new and good.

Honeymoons

The honeymoon is nearly over. We spent a glorious week on Guernsey where we cycled, swam, and joined a sea kayaking expedition. I'd like to sound brave and sporty about that last one but when the wind pushed me sideways, I confess that I panicked. My mind ran riot for a few dramatic seconds as I imagined being swept away and spending years on a desert island. That seemed tragic as I'd only just got married but luckily I was rescued by our competent, young leader, Skip. He tethered my kayak to his, and towed me through the tricky bits.

One of the best moments of the holiday was when we stood high above a tiny bay late at night. The Channel stretched out ahead and the full moon was reflected in rippling, golden stripes – a true honey moon.

Now we're back home and as we want to make the most of our remaining time off, we've decided to spend three days walking a section of the South West Coast Path. This trail is a much bigger project than the North Downs Way and is arguably the most challenging treat on my list. It's 630 miles and the total ascent is equivalent to climbing Mount Everest four times. If you're a head-banging kind of walker you could complete it in thirty days but I'm not in any rush and want to relish walking alongside the sea in Dorset, Devon, Cornwall and Somerset. It's going to require an unspecified number of trips to the South

West, each one delving deeper into the peninsula and getting further away from home. An added bonus is that it passes through the area where I grew up and this is a chance to see it with an adult perspective. I may even make my peace with it.

Most people start in Minehead and walk anti-clockwise round to Poole. I'm not sure why, and the South West Coast Path Association doesn't seem to know why either, but that's the way the guidebooks are written. The Association has produced a helpful Reverse Guide although the name does imply a regrettable deviation from the norm. Anyway, deviation or not, that's the way I'm doing it and I started out a few months ago, doing day trips from home. My friend Sheila was great company on the first stretch from South Haven Point to Swanage and after that Mike started joining me. He had initially said (slightly sniffily if I'm honest…) that he 'would come on some of the walks but wouldn't promise to do them all.' That suited me fine as it's definitely *my* project and I want to sort out all the logistics. But rather to his surprise, he quickly got hooked and we've developed a good rhythm when we walk – sometimes chatting, and other times walking separately for hours in quiet contemplation.

We're now too far into Dorset to do day trips so I book a few nights at a guesthouse in Abbotsbury. It's close to an open-top bus route. On the first morning we spend several hours walking along Chesil Beach next to the Fleet Lagoon. We have the beach almost to ourselves and the scenery looks like a Chinese watercolour. Mountains of pebbles rise up to our left and we spot three cormorants sitting motionless in a wooden rowing boat.

The only problem as the day wears on is that we've forgotten to bring our hats. We've run out of water too, and the sun is fierce as we follow the path off the beach and up steep, exposed slopes. Eventually it turns inland and we are overjoyed when we see a sign advertising a village pub. It's just half a mile away. Every step hurts as we limp along but as we reach our oasis and step through the big oak door, the lights go off. 'We close at three today,' says the landlord sounding grumpy. 'And it's five past.' We peer through the gloom at him, and he peers back at us. I'm ready for a standoff but we must look pitiful as he relents and says he will serve us drinks but we have to drink them outside. He sells us a pint of IPA and a ginger beer, and we slump against the wooden fence in the deserted garden.

The next day we trudge along the beach for miles. It's hard work on the pebbles but once again there's hardly anyone around despite it being summer. Great flocks of gulls gather by the water's edge, and as we get near, they take off providing spectacular aerial displays.

It's late afternoon by the time we get to West Bay where the cliff towers above us, steep and golden like an Egyptian sphinx. We swim and then we explore the small resort. I was expecting it to be staid and faded but instead we find ourselves eating wonderful fresh fish at a cool bar furnished in a salvage-gone-mad kind of way with red rusty metal rafters and techno music.

The third day is different again with lots of ups and downs. I puff my way unhappily up the first one and realise that I need a better strategy. Golden Cap, the highest point on the South Coast looms as an after-lunch challenge so I try a new approach – thirty steps then rest for five breaths, and so on. It's remarkably effective and I reach the top having barely broken into a sweat. I also make some new friends on the way. A young couple are just behind on the uphill slog, and when I tell them about my new discovery, they look pleased. From then on, every time I pause, I look back to see them standing still as they concentrate earnestly and puff out their cheeks. It reminds me of an antenatal class.

At Charmouth the tide is out and we walk across the seaweed. Bright green sea lettuce and a variety that resembles magenta mohair. It's like walking through wet salad. Then we pass a row of beach huts painted in tasteful beige and cream. 'I've never understood what they're for,' says Mike. 'I suppose they'd be OK if you like camping in a wardrobe.'

'You're so rude,' I say and laugh.

Slow living

When we get back from honeymoon, Molly and I move into Mike's house. She has a busy summer with friends and in September the three of us drive to London and her university hall of residence. As we unload her belongings from the car, she is excited and delighted that after many years of watching her siblings, she can at last join them in seizing her independence. And I am thankful that this is the last time I will have to go through the raw, gut-wrenching, rushed goodbye that signals the end of childhood.

She settles in quickly and sends regular updates. I, too, am settling into a different environment and establishing new routines. As always in recent years, I look to my list for distraction and realise that of the original sixty treats there are now just twelve that have, as yet, had no attention. And I have two and a half years in which to do them. Some of these involve significant travel and were put on the list optimistically with no idea when or how I would manage to do them – that's why they've been left so long. Then recently, completely out of the blue, I had a small windfall when a friend left me some money. I am still not sure whether I will get to the end of my list but at least I have the means to start planning.

For now though, I'm sticking to the simpler treats and it's a particular relief to have overcome my reading problem. I'm taking pleasure in books once more, and this means that at some point before long I'm going to have to read *Middlemarch*. It's a predictable inclusion in lists of significant fiction and is frequently called 'the greatest of the great Victorian novels.' At school I enjoyed *Silas Marner* but I've neglected Eliot's masterpiece until now. It's on my list simply because I'm curious about it.

I'm looking forward to getting started but have some apprehension. A book club blog made the national press recently when it advised 'Avoid *Middlemarch* at all costs. It is the death knell for a book club. Someone will confess "I've never read Dickens" and it's only a short hop from there until "we should try the classics" rears its fearful head. Attempt anything pre-1900 and over 450 pages and your book club will shrivel up and die.'

I can see why book groups – so often made up of people with busy lives who are trying to fit more into their busy lives– might find the heft of *Middlemarch* a tad daunting. It has thirty characters and my edition is just short of seven hundred pages. But fortunately, I'm not constrained by a book group schedule. It was not written to be read in a rush and deserves slow, reflective engagement. The trouble is that I don't know how to do things slowly. I'm not sure if I'm ready for *Middlemarch*.

Rushing is such a normal state for me that it's an effort to stand back and question it. And when I do, I get embroiled in an internal debate. Back and forth like a game of tennis. The players are Inquisitive Me who is all for improvement and Defensive Me who much prefers the status quo. IM asks awkward questions. But DM is well primed and bolshy. 'It's just who I am. Get used to it.' And I have to agree that my self-image is indeed of someone who likes to get things done and to squeeze in as much as possible. As I lie in bed at night drifting off to sleep, I go over the minutiae of the day and count up all the individual things I've done. I'm always asleep before I run out. Being productive helps me to feel worthwhile and purposeful. 'Live deep and suck out all the marrow of life,' as Henry David Thoreau said.

'Ah,' replies IM. 'That's all very well but I don't recall him saying that you have to rush.'

'There's an easy answer to that one,' responds Ms. Defensive. 'Many things are boring. Get them done as quick as possible.'

'Hang on a minute,' says IM, refusing to be silenced. 'It's not that straightforward. Have you ever noticed that you rush through the tedious stuff in order to get onto the more interesting things. But...as soon as you get to them, they redefine themselves as tedious, and so you hurry along to get to the more interesting things as soon as you can. That doesn't really make sense, does it?'

'Ah but there's such a lot to do. I have to go fast to get it all done.'

'Not really,' comes the rational response. And it's undeniably true. There were many years when I *was* genuinely busy keeping all the family balls in the air but no longer, as the children spread themselves across both geographical distance and adult life.

My justifications are not standing up to scrutiny. For me, rushing is a deeply-ingrained habit – a response to a dread of emptiness. My mother had it too. It's true that she had a busy working life but even when she retired, she would have urgent washing to hang out or pressing cupboards to tidy. She was impatient, too, with people who weren't as quick as her. 'Oh, *them*,' she'd say, 'They're too slow to catch a cold.' She'd laugh as she said it, but I knew it wasn't a compliment. The haste infection seems to have been passed on by me, too. 'I think I take after you, Mum,' said Molly recently. I glowed with maternal pride, and then she said, 'I'm very slapdash.'

The question remains – Does it matter if I rush? And will the habits that I have unwittingly passed on to the next generation, cause them damage? Should I warn them? Unfortunately, now that I've got my teeth into this, I'm pretty convinced that the answer to all of those questions is 'Yes.' There are *multiple* reasons why rushing is not a good idea. The first is that haste does undeniably make me slapdash as Molly is all too aware. This is generally not a good thing although it does have its compensations. Mike complains that when I load the dishwasher it looks as though I've hurled things in from the other side of the kitchen – they come out dirtier than when they went in. That one's easy. I just leave it to him.

The second is that I miss out on enjoying the present as I live with perpetual anticipation of the future. I've spent so much of my life wanting things to go faster. Steve Taylor puts it very well in his book *Back to Sanity*. 'When you rush, your mind is already in the future, and the present is just an inconvenience that stops you getting there.'

Thirdly, rushing makes me stressed and that's not good for anyone's health. It's quite possibly a contributory factor in my three chronic problems – migraines, early hours insomnia, and gastric reflux. There's even a name for it. In the 1950s two cardiologists noticed that many of the patients presenting with cardiovascular disease were in a continuous struggle and unremitting attempt to accomplish or achieve more and more things, or participate in more and more events in less and less time. They called it hurry sickness.

Fourth comes the problem of multi-tasking. If I cook dinner, send a few texts, listen to the radio, and build in some exercise at the same time, then that has always seemed super-efficient. Until now – it turns out that multi-tasking is a lot less efficient than people believe. It's only possible to focus on one task at a time so if you're juggling several activities, there's a constant process of swapping between them. This swap takes only tenths of a second but it's energy sapping and many studies have found that repeated switching reduces effectiveness. The net result is of attention spread thinly across a number of tasks. Many of us live in a constant state of what has been called *continuous partial attention* made infinitely worse by technology.

The fifth reason is also linked to reduced effectiveness. Studies of crowd behaviour have found that people get out through an exit more slowly when they rush. Slower and steadier is better than rushing. Sometimes my head is bursting with thoughts that all clamour to be dealt with at the same time and recently I've tried adopting a different strategy. 'Form an orderly queue,' I say to the thoughts in my head. 'You'll each get your turn.' And it does indeed help.

Sixth, rushing produces a feeling of shortage rather than satisfaction. There is nowhere to go with the feeling that there's not enough time because when you constantly fill it up with things to do then you'll never get it all done.

Last but far from least – rushing creates impatience and that means having less time for relationships. I always felt my mother was rushing too much to have time for me. It made her irritable and I would hate for my children to feel the same about me.

Sometimes it's good to go fast but it's the addiction that's the problem. I've surprised myself with the weight of evidence in favour of addressing this. And I'm not alone. Now that I've started on this path, I discover a huge range of material advocating the benefits of slowing down and being more intentional. This includes *In Praise of Slow*. The writer Carl Honoré was shocked into writing this when he was tempted by a book that offered a bedtime story he could read to his children in one minute. I read about slow food – local, sustainable ingredients, thoughtfully prepared with flavour and traditional cuisines in mind. Then there's slow media which challenges the standard values of rapid production, big audiences, and short attention span, by producing high-quality output for considered consumption. The iconic slow TV programme is Norwegian TV's seven-hour film of the Bergen to Oslo rail trip. Then there's slow eating. If you practise this, you're less likely to overeat as it takes fifteen minutes for your stomach to signal that you've eaten too much. All of this is mindfulness under a different label.

I experiment with what should be the easiest thing in the world – doing nothing. I generally wake up earlier than Mike and so I go to the spare room and sit in bed looking out at the trees. It challenges that nag that makes me feel I need to be purposeful and busy at all times. And it's a revelation to discover how hard I find it.

I also take the advice of Slow Movement writers and try to focus on one thing at a time. The general recommendation is to start by changing just one activity a day. I try slow ironing...slow toothbrushing...slow walking...slow supermarket shopping... slow weeding...slow chewing. But none of it comes easily. They're all sabotaged by my insatiable itch to get onto the next thing. Then I discover slow showering and that's much more successful. The warm water feels delicious, the soap smells fresh, and the shower tiles are scratchy under my feet. The oncoming day tries to force its way in but I'm not willing to greet it. I enlist an army of physical sensations to keep guard on my mindfulness. The towel is rough and as I pull it back and forth across my back, I think of a pig at a scratching post. I smooth rose-scented body cream over my legs which are inclined to get dry and as I do so, I think warmly of my friend Tilly who gave it to me for my birthday. It feels good to take care of myself and to be grateful for this body that has served me so well – producing four children and carrying me around at top speed for decades with very few complaints.

There's another new activity too, which takes me by surprise. As an adult I've never seen the point of jigsaws but when I visit a friend and see one laid out it reminds me that they were a favourite childhood activity. I had one that was a map of India scattered with cobras, tigers, the Taj Mahal, and water buffalo which all seemed very exciting in my quiet English surroundings. I did it over and over again. I order a 500-piece jigsaw of a harbour. There are different coloured buildings and unusual shapes in the picture and as I sit and work on it, I recapture that slow, meditative state of absorption that I have rarely enjoyed since childhood.

Maybe I am ready to try slow reading.

Maybe I am ready for *Middlemarch*.

Provincial life

I nibble at it in a quiet room for just ten or fifteen minutes at a time, and I return to it regularly. I know it will take me a few months to read but I keep in mind that the reading is the point *not* the getting through it. Otherwise, I will never find the insight that I'm looking for. I listen to some sections as an audiobook and the change in medium helps to stop me from feeling bogged down, and gives a different perspective on some of the characters.

I know so little at the outset that I have no idea what its title means. But Middlemarch is the name of a fictional Midlands town – the natural choice for George Eliot who was herself born in Nuneaton and spent her early adulthood in Coventry. Subtitled *A study of provincial life*, the many characters move in and out of one another's lives without a single hero or heroine at the centre.

George Eliot strove to write realistically and in 1856 she set out some of her principles in an essay called Silly Novels by Lady Novelists. It was published anonymously in the Westminster Review and she used it to criticise the majority of fiction written for and by women. She said that the world of these 'mind and millinery novels' is deeply unrealistic with beautiful, virtuous heroines making splendid marriages to rich, handsome husbands. Far from seeing these books as harmless entertainment, she argued that they were inflicting real damage by undermining the cause of education for women. Many of these female characters have had the benefit of a good education but they fail to make use of it. It's easy to see why Mary Ann Evans who wanted to be taken seriously, would choose to distance herself from women's novels by taking a male pseudonym.

She was known to have admired Jane Austen's wit so her criticisms are not aimed in that direction. But she was a very different kind of novelist and from the beginning of *Middlemarch* it's clear that we're a long way from the Austenian world of landed heroes, tidy plot resolutions and heaven-made marriages. I find it easier to relate to. We meet a number of married couples. A few are settled and content but others have serious tensions – generous-spirited versus cold...serious versus empty-headed... young versus old. The reasons why these characters have entered into unhappy marriages are no less likely today than they were then. Any of us could be misled by blind admiration, sexual attraction despite intellectual incompatibility, or otherwise have our heads turned in the quest for love, protection or status. Through the narrator, we learn of the many ways in which the characters misunderstand one another, and we see things from various points of view.

As in real life, there are many things that are not neatly resolved by the end. George Eliot was in her early fifties when she wrote it and by then had plenty of life experience to draw on. She'd suffered several bouts of depression, had appalled her father by rejecting religion, and after his death she moved to London to further her writing ambitions. After an unrequited romantic interlude, she eventually met her soulmate, the critic and philosopher George Henry Lewes. They adored one another but unfortunately, he was already married with three sons, and divorce was out of the question due to a legal quirk. This was in spite of the fact that his wife Agnes had four other children with her lover. Undeterred, they set up home together in 1854 even though their friends and family were scandalised. It was not unusual at that time to have adulterous affairs but theirs was different because they refused to conduct it in secrecy. He encouraged her to develop her writing and it was in tribute to him that she chose George for her pseudonym. It also helped to conceal her unusual domestic arrangements. At first George Eliot was thought to be a clergyman but after the success of *Adam Bede* when someone else claimed to be her, she owned up. By 1863 she was famous and had earned enough money to buy a beautiful house in Regent's Park. With this acclaim came better acceptance of her private life and even Queen Victoria, with all her moral prickles, was an admirer.

Middlemarch was published in 1872 but was set forty years prior to that. It can therefore portray enormous changes from a position of distance but still with enough proximity to make realistic observations. The characters are living through a period of rapid industrial development and we see how that impacts on individual lives and the settled community of this provincial town. We read of cholera outbreaks, reforming acts of Parliament, the coming of the railway, and the death of George IV. The individual facets of history are unique to that period but people's responses are relatable. As the railway develops, the landowners are keen to make money by selling off land, the workers worry about how it will affect their lives, and there is widespread suspicion about the health hazards of travelling at previously unimagined speed.

After George Eliot's death in 1880 she gradually fell out of favour and by the early twentieth century she was, in some quarters, the subject of derision. Lytton Strachey of the Bloomsbury Group considered her earnest and outdated. But it was another member of that difficult-to-please group who started her rehabilitation. In 1919, Virginia Woolf wrote an essay that famously called *Middlemarch* 'a magnificent book which with all its imperfections is one of the few English novels written for grown-up people.'

By the time I reach the end after several months of slow reading, I am very glad to have read it. I'm already curious to read it again, as I'm sure that I missed plenty on this first attempt. There were many passages that benefited from careful reading and from time to time wise words would simply leap out at me, so subtle in their phrasing, and capturing like Shakespeare, timeless aspects of human life. It's hard to choose from amongst so many but I particularly like 'Destiny stands by sarcastic with our dramatis personae folded in her hand.' I look back over the decades and remember how my life has taken me by surprise, not at all like I imagined it would be when I was young.

I can't claim to have slowed down very much but I am at least more aware of it, and know that it is possible and even enjoyable at times. I regret now that I made the children rush so much – even though fast walking gave them wonderfully strong legs – and I've talked to them about my efforts to slow down. Maybe if I have grandchildren the generational cycle will be reprogrammed.

There's a lesson here too in recognising that it's not always possible to see things clearly at first. Patience is a virtue but

I've not been very good at resisting the temptation to jump to conclusions and instead to let things unfold in their own time. You cannot rush the process of accepting, adapting and all the other things that accompany change.

In the meantime, the good news is that Molly does at least *notice* when things are too fast. That's a first step. She recently acquired a smart record player and is busy building up a vinyl collection. She's home from university for the weekend and appears to be enjoying her new turntable. But things aren't going as well as I thought, and eventually she emerges from her room, looking very downcast. 'Everything sounds so *fast*,' she says unhappily. From the benefit of my relatively long life, I am able to enlighten her about the all-important difference between 45rpm and 33rpm.

Finding It

Since moving into Mike's house, I've been thinking about the meaning of home. This is my seventh home in eleven years and a lot has happened in that time. The upside is that I've become efficient at packing and unpacking removal boxes but this skill is outweighed by the many downsides of feeling unrooted. I want all the packing and unpacking to stop. I'd like to feel settled – at last.

This new home is in an unremarkable suburban street where people tend to keep themselves to themselves. But there is much to like about it. It's a sanctuary where I can recharge my batteries, a palette board on which to express our tastes and identities, and a place in which to have fun and to care for the people we love. One of the best things about growing up has been creating homes that feel bright, safe and comfortable.

That *should* all be good but I find it hard to relax and simply enjoy what I have. I've heard avid gardeners say the same about their gardens. *Just sitting* is difficult when you're surrounded by things that clamour to be deadheaded, pruned, or expunged. My indoor equivalent is that when I settle down to relax, I fidget – jumping up to adjust the curtains, to straighten a picture that has gone askew, or to swipe at a cobweb. Mike's unfazed by half-open drawers and cupboard doors. I *have* to shut them. Monica in *Friends* would understand. And my mind keeps wandering off to explore possibilities. If I just painted that wall a different colour…if I could just find the right plant for that corner…if I just repositioned this…just tweaked that… Omnipresent is a seductive image of that magic moment when everything will be in harmony – the wooden floors sweet with polish, cheerful vases of tulips dotted around, the biscuit tin filled with home-made offerings, birdsong drifting through the spotless open windows, and snowy-white curtains gently wafting in the breeze. '*Then,*' I think. '…*then* life will be perfect and I will be truly contented.' But until that moment arrives, I will have to wait.

For years I justified this delayed gratification mindset as a consequence of the everyday chaos of family life. And more recently, as I can no longer blame the children, I've attributed it to feeling rootless.

I know that I *should* be content as I have immensely more than most of the world's population could ever dream of. More too, than my mother ever had. It's the inability to rein in my imagination that causes so much of the unrest. I've learned not to look at home magazines as they just fuel the desire for perfection. That's their job. But I fall prey to it in other ways. Recently, I stayed with a friend and appreciated the pretty pink glasses next to the bed, so much more pleasing than my cheap Ikea ones. And her soap dishes were *so* charming…

It was Bob Marley who said, 'Money is numbers and numbers never end. If it takes money to be happy, your search for happiness will never end.' That applies equally to the restless attitude I bring to my surroundings. The potential for change is limitless. How will I *know* when everything is just right? Do I really have to wait for the mythical snowy-white curtains?

I'm drawn to the Danish concept of hygge as articles about it are always accompanied by photos of candles, flickering fires, warm socks, stylish mugs, cake, and laughing people in woolly hats. I've learned how to pronounce it – *hooga* – but it's elusive, and reading about it only leaves me envious and puzzled.

There *is* one thing though that sums up home for me and that's the steady tick-tock of a clock. When I was a teenager and had my first boyfriend, I often used to stay with his parents in Edinburgh. They had lived in their comfortable Morningside villa for many years and it felt stable and content. I loved coming back after an evening out when the house was dark and the only sound was the ticking of their old clock, a heartbeat at the centre of everything, reassuring and homely. I've carried that memory with me for years and so it was that capturing the sensuousness of a steady tick and deep chimes made it to my list. I thought initially that Shaun's granny's clock would fit the bill but after the Winchester Cathedral debacle I realised it was beyond resurrection.

Unknown to me, in the case of this particular treat then serendipity is waiting in the wings. Or more precisely it's waiting in the loft. One of the things that Mike and I have been doing as we set up our new merged life is to go through the things in his roof space. It's been a long time since he looked at what is there. We peer into cardboard box after cardboard box, and inside one is an oak mantle clock. It doesn't look particularly exciting and Mike can't remember where it came from. Or even if it works. But it *is* a clock.

We wind it. We give a little push on the pendulum and it moves back and forth a few times, and then stops. We try again. But it doesn't want to play. That's probably why it's been in a box for all these years and so it sits for several more months in a corner of the hall while we wonder what to do with it.

Then one morning I wake up with a rush of enthusiasm. I look on the British Horological Institute website to find the nearest accredited clockmaker, put the clock in a shopping bag, and drive across the city to a dark little shop in uncharted territories.

The clockmaker wears fine wire-rimmed glasses and looks as though he has been in his shop for several centuries. He doesn't say much at first but fiddles deftly in the belly of the clock. 'Is it worth repairing?' I ask. 'And how much will it cost?'

'I can certainly get it working,' he says. 'It will be about three hundred and fifty pounds.'

'Hmm,' I say, as I can't think of anything more sensible. We chat for several minutes about similar clocks that he has mended and I start to adjust to the idea of spending quite a bit of money.

Then he holds up his finger and whispers, 'Listen.' And in amongst all the various tick-tocks in the shop I hear a mellow tick-tock right in front of me. He delves back inside. 'And *now* listen.' There is a pleasing sound of mechanical whirring and anticipatory positioning and then the clock strikes nine. It doesn't matter that it's actually ten past eleven. What matters is that I like the sound very much.

'Look,' he says. 'I'll be honest with you. I'm very busy at the moment. Several other clockmakers in the area have retired so it might take me a couple of months to get around to yours. But I think you might find that it's alright – it's still ticking. Strap it into the car. Be sure to use the seatbelt and see how you get on. You can always bring it back to me.'

So that's what I do. I take it home and place it on the mantelpiece in the sitting room. I set the pendulum going again and move the hands carefully until they are synchronised with the chimes. When Mike gets back at the end of the day it is still ticking away – a new, comfortable presence in our home.

Several months pass and it's doing well, although I've nursed it through minor ailments with phone advice from the clockmaker, and I do confess to having fussed it quite a bit. It turned out not to be completely happy on the mantelpiece as that had a slight slope. So I moved it to the ledge in the bay window. But then I worried that it would get cold at night. And I couldn't see it when the curtains were drawn. Its next move was to a small side-table in the corner of the room where it looked ungainly and out of proportion. Then at last I found the perfect spot – the hall table – and that's where it lives now, right at the centre of the house. I walk past it umpteen times each day and that reminds me to wind it and talk to it regularly. It ticks steadily, with ninety-six announcements a day – polite quarter-hour chimes and then big enthusiastic bongs on the hour. But it does lose about ten minutes a week, and I've had to prop its left foot up on a fifty-pence piece otherwise the pendulum stops. So it looks a bit tipsy.

Alongside my love affair with the imperfect clock, I'm beginning to see that my long-held restlessness has had little to do with the actual spaces I've called home. They've been comfortable, well-appointed and adequately clean. It's been my *expectations* of them that have got in the way. I've wanted them to make me feel stable and serene. But perhaps it doesn't work like this. Maybe it has to be the other way round. Feel stable and serene inside and then you feel happier in your environment.

One morning I wake up early and go downstairs to make a cup of tea and a hot water bottle. The garden is ablaze with autumn colour but I'm not ready for that yet and slip into the spare bedroom where I can read without disturbing Mike. I settle down under the duvet and put my feet on the hot water bottle. I've just started a new Ann Patchett novel and I'm enjoying it very much. There's the pleasant anticipation of breakfast – warming porridge drizzled with maple syrup and dusted with cinnamon. My family are with me in the photos on the bookcase and the flowery hot water bottle cover that Emma sewed for me.

The clock strikes seven.

Suddenly from nowhere comes the word *hygge*. 'This is hygge,' I say out loud. 'I've found it.'

This particular morning is not remarkable in any way. Other than that, I feel content. I'm thinking about what is right rather than what is wrong. I have what I need. And for once, I know it.

I carry on reading, knowing that this has been a significant moment.

Flamingos

Now that all the children are either fully or partially fledged there is not the day-to-day contact that I once took for granted. Family gatherings are – mostly – lovely but I also value their company individually and a perfect opportunity presents itself when Emma leaves her job and takes a break while trying to decide what to do next. I've been wanting to visit the Camargue and am thrilled when she says she'd like to join me on the trip that I have planned for early December.

This ended up on the list because I want to see flamingos in the wild – in their desolate salty lagoons. And we don't need to go to Lake Titicaca or the Great Rift Valley. Instead, a short haul flight to Marseille will get us most of the way to the Camargue National Park, the biggest river delta in Western Europe and a favourite nesting place for these strange, leggy birds.

We meet up at Heathrow and as we walk along interminable corridors, I do my best to keep up with my daughter who glides along serenely looking efficient and cosmopolitan as she wheels her suitcase next to her. 'I wish *my* suitcase would do that,' I say.

'It does,' she replies. And shows me. I take to it quickly and immediately feel efficient and cosmopolitan. From now on I shall never again be a straggly tourist lumbering along with my luggage and tripping everyone up. And I will think of Emma tenderly every time I do this. Later, as the plane soars into the clear winter sky her hand comes across and takes mine. She's done plenty of flying both for work and pleasure but despite all of this practice she still doesn't like it. I'm not sure if the hand is there to comfort me or her, but I don't ask and it doesn't matter.

From Marseille we get a train to Arles and then we walk alongside the Rhône to our accommodation. It's a small, tall, cream house with wooden shutters and it's all ours for the next three days. The cobbled street is so narrow that if we stood in the middle with our arms outstretched, we could touch the houses on either side. The owner is there to greet us and with her English, my French, and Emma chipping in with some Spanish, we manage a friendly conversation.

Next morning we agree that we both slept pretty well but were a bit cold. And when I go outside to pin back our shutters, an icy blob settles on my nose. It's snowing and the mistral is blowing. Here we are in the South of France, and the temperature is several degrees lower than in England.

The market is reputed to be one of the best in France so we set off to explore, and on our way, we nip into a pharmacy to buy a couple of hot water bottles. The assistant smiles. '*Il ne neige jamais!*' she exclaims. Today's drama is only a light flurry but we're unsure whether to feel lucky to have a brush with such an unusual phenomenon or unfortunate to be having a chilly weekend. We stroll past market stalls loaded with local goats' cheeses; lavender honey; wooden bowls of green, black and violet olives; fish; patisserie, and Provençal tomatoes.

The stallholders lean away from the customers, hunched inside hoods. As usual Emma is better prepared than me and is bundled up in a scarf and gloves. But I'm freezing and so we stop at a stall selling woollen shawls. I select a pale grey one and drape it tentatively around my shoulders. It's wonderfully warm and comforting. No wonder sheep can cope with wintry fields. I take it off and hand the gruff stallholder ten euros. There's no need for a bag as it's going straight back on. At this moment it feels like the best piece of clothing I've ever owned. I wrap it around me with a flourish and feeling like Marilyn Monroe, wait for my daughter's approval. 'Are you alright, Mum?' she says. 'You look a bit flushed.'

The following day we go to pick up our hire car. The office is in a quiet side street on the far side of town, in amongst car repair workshops, vape stores and tired laundrettes, and I'm dreading this bit. At home I'm a confident-enough driver but some years ago I had an unhappy mishap in France, and it's left me with a fear of driving abroad. I'd assumed we would be able to get round on public transport but discovered when researching the trip that in winter there's no way to explore the marshlands other than by car. Emma was with me when I had my bad experience and knows that I'm anxious. She's not got a driving licence yet as she lives in London and has no need but despite that she's the grown-up here. We get into our compact Renault and she immediately takes control, checking the route on her phone and giving me clear directions.

We make our way through the city and at every junction I brace myself for a crash and try not to cry. Thankfully neither of those things happen and it's not long before we're on the D36B heading south. The road is empty and flat as we pass vineyards and fields of corn, asparagus and rice. The sky is vast and overcast but there's no further snow. Intriguing little farm tracks lead off the main road, and then on our right we see the Étang de Vaccarès, the biggest of the Camargue lagoons.

'Look!' shouts Emma urgently, pointing up. 'Stop!'

I pull over and there above us is our first flamingo – with a pink tutu body. Neck stretched out, slender legs like a dart – scarlet and black wings flapping. This is an intensely exciting moment and we are silent as we take it in.

We watch until the bird is out of sight and then continue on our journey to La Capelière where we need to buy tickets for the nature reserve. Most Camargue flamingos fly to Africa for the winter but around five thousand decide to remain in France so there should be plenty for us to see. A bonus is that they're particularly flamboyant at this time of year, with colourful new plumage all ready for their courtship displays. The visitor centre is in an old farmhouse and the parking area is almost deserted today.

The website mentions that the staff have a deep commitment to helping tourists enjoy their visit and as we enter, we are immediately greeted by a serious lady in a forest-green cardigan. 'Two tickets, please,' I say in my best French.

She puts her head on one side and looks us up and down. 'Where do you want to go?' she asks.

'We want to see the flamingos,' I say.

She gives us directions to the lagoon and tells us that the board-walk trail will take us to the best viewing points. 'And what will you do then?' she asks in English.

'We will visit the saltworks,' I reply still managing to keep up in French.

'And after that?' she says.

'We will drive to a restaurant for lunch,' I say.

'And after that?'

Emma giggles. 'We will return to Arles,' I reply.

'And after that?'

'We will go home and sleep,' I say, laying my head on my arms and closing my eyes. At *last*, she hands us our tickets.

This park feels entirely natural but is in fact a man-made habitat created with the aim of attracting flamingos as well as curlews, grey herons, little egrets, stilts, and avocets. It's a place where fragile wildlife and not-at-all fragile humans can spend time close to one another, and it's not long before we see flocks of flamingos with their haughty Roman beaks. Some stand on one leg which saves energy as they use fewer muscles to stay upright. Others appear to sit with their knees bent and their legs stretched forwards. But the joints in their legs and feet are not what they seem. Their knees are actually tucked away out of sight under their body feathers, and the joint that is so obvious in the middle of their long legs is their ankle. The stretch from the middle of their leg to the end of their toes is all one big foot.

There are many things about flamingos that are unusual, and one is that the parents feed their single chick with a rich milk that they regurgitate. The only other birds that do this are pigeons and male emperor penguins. The chicks have grey feathers and it takes about four years for them to get their distinctive pink colouring. This comes from carotenoids in the saltwater shrimp and algae that they eat. The pinkest flamingos are the ones that attract mates, probably because colour indicates to potential mates that the individual bird is well-nourished. It seems curious that diet has such an effect on colouring and I consider myself lucky not to have been permanently stained by all the beetroot and sunset-yellow Lucozade I craved each time I was pregnant.

Our next stop is about ten miles south – the salt pans at Salin-de-Giraud where we climb up onto a raised observation platform and gaze out in awe over pink lakes that look like dentist's mouthwash. On the far side are huge white mountains of salt, and mechanical diggers. It feels bizarre and trippy. This salt will eventually be sold for de-icing roads and is produced by pumping seawater into the man-made ponds from where it crystallises out through evaporation. The water is pink thanks to pigmented, salt-loving bacteria.

From there it's a short drive to a small roadside restaurant that's recommended in our guidebook. The patron greets the guests ahead of us with a duet of kisses and extravagant bonhomie. We get a warm welcome but no kisses and he settles us at a table overlooking shady plane trees and a seemingly limitless expanse of field. Our hors-d'oeuvres are simple but perfectly balanced – spinach leaves, radicchio, long rosy radishes with lime green stalks, mushroom, sun-dried tomato and hard-boiled egg with a balsamic dressing. Emma has pork to follow and I have grilled sea bream which the waiter fillets deftly at the table.

As we wait for cheese and fruit, Emma circles her hand around the tall stem of her wineglass. 'I want to feel valuable,' she says. Fear wakes up instantly, always on alert. I worry about my children making mistakes that will harm them or make their lives more difficult than they have to be. But she's an adult now and I have to hold back from my instinctive need to make everything better. This is not about cuddles and plasters and I know that she will find her own way through this career quandary. Even so, I could not feel happier that she's talking to me about it. I wouldn't have felt able to do that with *my* mother.

2017

A better understanding

It's Friday. It also happens to be my birthday. Not the big one by which time I want to have completed all the treats – that's still two years away. But it's a birthday nonetheless and there's no lie-in or even tea in bed. Instead, two alarms wake us at five o'clock and we open the curtains onto an inky February morning. Half an hour later we're out of the door with overnight bags. No need for breakfast as we'll be having that four hundred miles away. Living ten minutes from a regional airport has its advantages.

By nine o'clock we're at Lily's Cafe in the centre of Dublin ordering scrambled eggs and smoked salmon. There's plenty of time for the newspapers, and today there are yet more stories about Brexit and Trump. I turn to the crossword instead and a little later, fortified by several coffee refills we walk down O'Connell Street, cross the Liffey and pass through Front Gate into the huge, cobbled quadrangle of Ireland's most prestigious university. There we spot a thin young man with a large umbrella. This is our walking-tour guide and he's already deep in conversation with the other two members of our group. He's a postgrad history student and as he welcomes us to Trinity College, he explains that it was founded by Queen Elizabeth I in 1592 and that its official name is the College of the Holy and Undivided Trinity of Queen Elizabeth near Dublin.

He promises that there will be more – much more – about Elizabeth and other English monarchs.

Then it's back to the congested streets as he whisks us through key events in Dublin's history. I know little about Ireland and so almost all of it is new to me. After an hour, we stop for coffee at the Irish Film Institute, a cosy respite from a torrential downpour. We squash round a small table – an Irishman, an American, a German, a South African and me – and we talk about the state of the world. We're united in our dismay at America's president and although we're in broad agreement about what else is good and bad in the news, it's thought-provoking to hear individual perspectives. It's a wrench to go back into the rain but there are still things our enthusiastic guide wants to show us. As we wander round, I can see that Dublin is a proud and attractive city but it's impossible to ignore the oppression that has shaped it.

The tour was billed as two hours, but as we approach the four-hour mark, I'm suffering from information overload and a lack of lunch so I nudge Mike. We nod silently to one another and excuse ourselves. Food is a high priority but it's hard to pass a good bookshop and once inside I'm waylaid by a pocket history of Ireland. The tour has highlighted how little I know about this country and I'm ashamed of my previous indifference. I buy the book and as we settle down in a cafe with a large pot of tea and a plate of scones, I begin to read.

Mike has bought a book about French history and that keeps him happy as rain hammers against the windows. Over the next hour I build up a rough understanding of things that have shaped Ireland. It's not surprising to find countless twists and turns, not least because of the many feuds and differences of opinion amongst the Irish themselves. But here – with apologies if your grasp of Irish history is better than mine – are a few facts that seem significant:

> *English monarchs have been gifting Irish land to their loyal English subjects since the reign of Henry II.*
>
> *In 1542 after breaking ties with the Vatican, Henry VIII feared that France and Spain would use Catholic Ireland as a base from which to invade England. So he appointed himself King of Ireland and Head of the newly protestant Church of Ireland – thereby beginning the religious division that has troubled Ireland ever since.*
>
> *In 1652 Oliver Cromwell's army drove thousands of Irish Catholics from their homes and the English Parliament confiscated their land.*
>
> *From the end of the seventeenth century, laws were introduced forbidding Catholic priests from preaching in Ireland and Great Britain, and banning the Gaelic language.*
>
> *Anyone sporting green items such as a ribbon or handkerchief could be imprisoned, transported or put to death, as could anyone found to have the self-seeding shamrock weed growing on their land. These were all seen as symbols of nationalistic pride.*
>
> *The Irish fought vigorously for independence in the late eighteenth century but their rebellion was crushed. Having lost its American colony, Britain was nervous and responded with the Act of Union in 1800 which created the United Kingdom of Great Britain and Ireland.*

> From 1845-1852, potato crop failure resulted in a million deaths from starvation. While people were starving, tons of grain and other Irish food products were exported to Britain.
>
> Gladstone believed that civil unrest would only be resolved when the Irish were granted self-rule. His Home Rule Bill was rejected in 1886 and 1893. A third attempt in 1912 succeeded but the timing was unlucky and implementation was put on hold for the duration of the First World War.
>
> During this war 200,000 Irishmen responded to Britain's cause and 30,000 of them died in action. Despite their loyalty, Kitchener said he 'would not trust one single Irishman with a rifle in his hand.'
>
> In 1916 a group of Irish Republicans – educated men including artists and poets – organised what became known as the Easter Rising. They laid siege to Dublin, declaring the right of the Irish people to ownership of Ireland. The leaders were executed by the British Army.

That's as far as I get today. Eventually the rain stops so we close our books and make our way out into the street, side-stepping puddles and swapping snippets of Irish and French history. It's just a short walk to our accommodation in the home of an artist named Niamh. Our room is white with bold splashes of peacock blue and butter yellow.

Next morning we take the bus to the former Kilmainham Gaol where the leaders of the Easter Rising were imprisoned and executed. We're not expecting cheerful stories. But the reality is even harsher than I imagined.

Afterwards we take a short walk to the Irish Museum of Modern Art and spend several hours in the formal gardens, wild meadows, and airy rooms. We particularly enjoy some Lucian Freud paintings, raw and challenging but offering up plenty to discuss.

In the evening we're booked onto a literary pub crawl so we wrap up warmly and walk through the shiny, wet streets to The Duke. We go upstairs as instructed and as we wait for something to happen, I feel a firm tap on my shoulder. 'Hello,' says a young man. 'Where are *you* from?' He shows real interest and says that he is 'up from Kildare for the evening.' He tells us about the difficulties of getting work in rural Ireland. Then at 7.15 on the dot, two actors arrive and over the next few hours they lead us through streets broad and narrow, and into three more pubs. They tell us about Dublin's famous literary figures. Wilde, Beckett, Yeats, Heaney, Shaw, Behan, and Joyce – they each get their moment. No mention of any women though, other than the odd wife or mistress. The tour ends at a fifth pub and we stay there till midnight, deep in conversation with a friendly Dublin couple. Once again, we find ourselves in a debate about the current state of the world. People are more unsettled than I can ever remember.

On Sunday morning we take in various sights including gorgeous Georgian terraces and the huge neoclassical General Post Office which was the headquarters of the Easter Rising. You can still see bullet holes in the wall. Opposite, is The Spire – a stainless steel cone and currently the world's tallest street sculpture. It replaced an imperial statue of Nelson that was bombed in 1966. People ask 'What does it commemorate? What's it for?' But it doesn't commemorate anything. It just points to the future.

There's so much more to see but we have to collect our bags and before we leave, Niamh invites us to share a pot of tea. We tell her about the walking tour and the pub crawl, and the interesting people we've met. I tell her, too, how glad I am to have learned something about Irish history. She smiles. Then the conversation moves to current world politics. Niamh says that she was in Maine just before the American election and was shocked to see the impact of recession. The small town where she was staying had recently lost most of its timber industry to Canadian competition and only a quarter of the shops were still in business. She makes it clear that she wouldn't vote for Trump, but she does say that after her visit she can see why many people want protectionist policies. 'We need to listen and try to understand both sides,' she says.

It's been a great weekend but it's left me feeling uneasy. How is it that I could have been so uninterested in this country's history? The obvious answer is that it didn't affect me personally. It was someone else's story so even when The Troubles were in the news, I paid little attention. And despite our countries being intertwined I don't remember my history teachers ever breathing the word *Ireland*. Like other aspects of colonialism, it just wasn't in the syllabus. Mike says it was the same for him in South Africa. Black history wasn't discussed.

This leads me to wonder whether it *matters* not to care. It's not like anyone in Ireland will have noticed my quiet indifference for all these years. But I've explored new territory this weekend and one key argument against indifference is that it allows bad things to slip in unchallenged. During Ireland's Great Famine it was power and economic greed that drove the political engines but at a human level there was denial, dehumanisation, and disinterest. There's still plenty of that in the world. And while social media is supposed to make us *better* connected it actually makes it easier to detach from people's problems and for that to spill into real-life relationships. Narcissism and self-promotion are paraded on TV and meanwhile the biggest narcissist of all has slipped into the White House.

When I've experienced understanding in my own life, I've been grateful and *I* want to be better at giving it. G*enerous listening* – not butting in with suggestions and platitudes just because that makes *me* feel better. And trying to understand how things are for the other person. Not how it might be for me if I were in that situation but how it is for *them*, with *their* unique history and personality. Which brings me to conclude that if you try to live by the values of empathy in your personal life then it's inconsistent to put those values aside and dump the rest of humankind in a different box.

My weekend in Dublin has given me plenty to think about. No-one can take on the problems of the world. No-one can care about everything but it's been discomfiting to realise just how ignorant I've been of problems so close to home.

Reframing

Months and months have passed since I started my art project with Claire. I see her socially several times but avoid committing to another painting date. My excuses are genuine. We're getting married. We're caring for my father-in-law. We're terribly busy. But underneath this fleece of evasion, I know that if I really wanted to, I would make time. The strength of my fear is perplexing. I know plenty of people who are scared of things. One will drive for miles to avoid travelling on a motorway. Another is afraid of water after her brother ducked her in a swimming pool decades ago. These fears centre around potential physical dangers and have some rational basis. All I'm being asked to do is to make some marks on a piece of white canvas.

Then one day when I'm visiting my friend Frances, I spot a book on her kitchen counter and after a cursory glance at the front cover, I flip it over and skim through the blurb. 'Any good?' I ask.

'Everyone's talking about it,' she says. And with limited precious time together we move swiftly on to exchange news. A couple of weeks later Emma comes to stay and tells me about a wonderful book she is reading, and how it has changed the way she views her potential. *Mindset*. It's the same one. I'm cautious about diving into self-help books. Too often they overpromise and underdeliver and the earnest encouragement makes me nauseous. But I know that amongst the heaving bookshop shelves, there are *some* that are genuinely useful, so based on the recommendations of two people whose opinions I value, I order it. And the author, Carol S Dweck is no lightweight. She's a psychology professor at Stanford.

It's easy to read and the message is fundamentally simple. Some people have fixed mindsets and others have growth mindsets. Those with a fixed mindset will avoid hard situations where they might expose their inadequacies and look stupid. Those with a growth mindset believe that they can change through effort and experience. They welcome challenge as an opportunity to learn.

A fixed mindset is all about measuring your talents and abilities as if they were set in stone. You're either good at something or you're not. When people do things apparently effortlessly, it's easy to value that. A parent might reinforce this by praising their child. 'You're *so* good at playing the piano.' But talent and ability are brittle when viewed like this. By seeming to be in fixed supply, the limit can be reached or you might trip and they might shatter. What then? Where do you go from there? If you seek validation from what you *can* do then you're in trouble. Growth on the other hand is not limited. Praising someone's commitment and effort will most likely encourage them to do more. And if you have never failed then are you really a success?

Dweck describes the moment that she realised she'd shifted from a fixed mindset to one of growth. Instead of thinking, 'This is hard. I'll stop,' she found herself thinking, 'This is hard. This is fun.'

This gives me a way to frame my artistic struggles. It helps to attach words to what was previously just a fog of emotion, and gives me something I can work with. It gives me the means to understand that I absorbed the message my mother gave me – our family is not artistic – and I plonked it straight down in a rigid fixing where the slightest gust would give me palpitations. That and the fear that if you do not judge your efforts accurately then people will laugh at you.

I'm still busy trying to make sense of all this, when Claire gets in touch. She's a committed teacher and committed teachers don't give up on their pupils, even the resistant ones. Maybe *particularly* the resistant ones. She slices cleanly through my reticence and tells me that she and her husband are coming to stay. Rick and Mike will go off to the Isle of Wight to take photos, and I will finish my painting.

We have a chatty evening, lingering at the table over fish pie and the next morning after breakfast we wave the boys off. It's just Claire, me and the painting. I'm armed with my newly-discovered growth mindset and all morning I draw and paint while Claire offers suggestions.

I know that I must try to enjoy the process and not think too much about the end product. When I ask Claire why she paints, she says that she loves the meditative quality. 'It's a bit like yoga. It demands a very high level of concentration and focus. I get transported when I'm painting and I love squirting the squidgy paint about and working with it.' She makes it sound fun.

'Enjoy it,' I think. 'Be playful.'

I try but it's still a struggle and I'm painfully aware of the gap between what I want to do and what I am able to produce today. We had a big breakfast so we skimp on lunch and finish up last night's blueberry and lemon tart. Then Claire gives a little yawn and says she's going upstairs for a nap.

'You can't leave me on my own with *this*,' I think. But I know that even with a good friend, I can't let this childish whine of abandonment escape, so I get on with painting the steam train instead. Copying from the photo I used last time, I start to fill in the lines like a colouring book. As carefully as I can. Red, black, brown. I'm absorbed. This is hard. This is almost fun.

Now that Claire is not here to tell me what to do next, I can either sit down and have a cup of tea or I can grasp ownership and move onto the next bit. I look for pictures of primroses. They're an important childhood memory. The Devon hedgerows were full of them in the Spring and I inhaled their unique delicate scent. Warm and musky with a hint of citrus. I copy them into several of my side panels. I've always thought that I was observant. After all, I'm the one who finds lost items in the house. I can conjure up a visual memory of where things are, especially when they're in the wrong place. It's a useful skill but rather joyless and managerial. This is different. I'm counting the petals and looking, really looking, at the ribs in the thick green leaves, and the subtle shading at the centre of the flowers.

Claire comes down and is surprised to see how much progress I've made. It's nearly finished. 'I know it's not very good,' I say compulsively. But at least I understand better why I feel I need to say that. I fill in the final panels with silvery tiddlers, church stained glass, and a flat plaice with pebbly camouflaged skin.

'It's lovely,' says Claire. I still can hardly bear to look at it but we agree that my next challenge is to take it to be framed and not claim that one of my children did it. I do manage this but only by being uncharacteristically monosyllabic. If I chat too much, I think the banned words might just slip out.

I heard a painter say on the radio, that the worst thing for an artist is when people just walk past their work. 'You want to stick a nine-inch nail through their foot and make them stay there as long as possible.' Mine looks better now it's framed, but I don't feel ready for wider viewing so I hang it in the bathroom where I can see it from the bath. I force myself to look at it and to my surprise within a few weeks, I feel less harshly judgemental and am even beginning to have quite fond thoughts towards it. I was capable of more than I thought. Certainly, more than my mother would have thought. And the truth is that people talk about it taking thousands of hours to master a skill –I only spent about twelve, at most.

I mention my thoughts to Claire. 'You were certainly resistant,' she said. 'But you really wanted to do it. Let me know if you want to do another.'

Spring rain

After our honeymoon we did a couple more sections of the South West Coast Path but took a break for the winter. I never mind walking in the rain but don't like the idea of narrow, high paths made slippy with frost. We've resumed again now that it's Spring and have had a couple of short expeditions. As each section gets further away from home it demands more commitment but setting off before dawn means that we can be at our starting point in time for a full day of walking. Today we're heading for Teignmouth from where we will take the train eastwards and walk back, and then tomorrow we will walk westwards. Mike drives for the first bit while I snooze, and then I take over. He snores quietly next to me as I drive through Wiltshire and Dorset and the sun comes up. I wonder what we will see on this trip. Every part of this walk brings its own minor adventures and unique character.

By ten we're in Teignmouth so we put on our boots and make our way to the station. When the train arrives, it has just two carriages, and every inch of space is packed with children, overstuffed rucksacks and group leaders, all on their way to a holiday camp at Dawlish Warren. We squeeze in and as we didn't have time to buy a ticket, I edge my way through the squash to find the conductor. On the way I tread on a sad-eyed Labrador's tail. His yelp makes everyone gasp and as I turn to apologise profusely to the dog and its owner, my rucksack bashes a woman in the face. Horrified, I turn back to apologise to her too, at which point Mike whispers urgently, 'Look!' And I remember how much I have wanted to show off this bit of my home county to him – this spectacular route through alternating tunnels in the cliffs and great views of the sea. I'd nearly missed it. Unlike a small child at the front of the carriage who sits on his mother's knee and chuckles as the train flashes in and out of the light. His uncomprehending pleasure reminds me of taking Will in a department store lift when he was a similar age. The door closed and when it opened again as if by magic onto an entirely different scene, he giggled with delight.

We get off the train at Starcross and then walk for miles beside the beach through Dawlish back to Teignmouth. We have the sea to our left and the railway to our right, with rattly local trains and sleek expresses passing at regular intervals. At one point we pass an old man hobbling along with a golden retriever by his side. It's carrying a pair of blue saddlebags on its back and looks conscientious and cheerful.

Later, after getting settled in our accommodation – by coincidence another artist's home – we set off to explore the local pubs. Teignmouth was once a fashionable watering hole and has a wide Georgian esplanade called Den Crescent. It's where fishing nets were laid out to dry, and it was also used for racing horses, donkeys and pigs. And as we walk along enjoying the mellow seaside light, we come across our third dog of the day. A teenage boy goes past with a Staffordshire bull terrier on a lead and a skateboard under his arm. Suddenly he jumps on the skateboard, still holding onto the lead and the dog gallops off at top speed. They are euphoric and the boy leans slightly forward in a remarkable display of trust and balance.

The next day is extremely wet and we start with a short ride in a small wooden boat across the River Teign to Shaldon—it's believed to be the oldest ferry service in the UK. We are the only passengers and the ferryman hands us a shower squeegee so that we can dry the slatted, varnished seats.

By lunchtime we are drenched and dripping. We sit high up on the cliffs with damp sandwiches and lukewarm coffee, looking out on the elephant-grey sea. Keats visited Teignmouth in 1818 and wrote to a friend about the 'abominable Devonshire Weather ... the truth is, it is a splashy, rainy, misty, snowy, foggy, haily, floody, muddy, slipshod county.' It certainly can be, but unlike Keats, I like rain and refuse to agree when people say, 'Isn't it *awful*.' It's got lots going for it. It's clean...you get the world to yourself...and there's a bit of drama. It does of course help to have modern water-resistant fabrics. Later, we reach a clearing surrounded by tall thin trees. The branches resemble rafters and join above us in an impromptu roof. 'It's a cathedral in the woods...' says Mike. '...and listen to the music of the rain...' I'd been feeling slightly guilty for loving this weather and dragging him out in it. But if I needed any reminder that he is the man for me, then this is it.

In the evening, we have a simple salad at a posh hotel in Shaldon with uninterrupted views over the river to Teignmouth. We watch as a ship approaches the entrance to the harbour. It moves steadily forwards and then abruptly stops and starts to go backwards. It manoeuvres itself into what might be a better position, and then it moves forwards again. Then it stops, drifts sideways and moves backwards once more. This doesn't seem right at all and the light is fading fast. My mind races. 'What will this unwieldy boat do once it's dark? Is it actually possible for it to get into the harbour?' It's really substantial and the potential gap for it to enter is quite small. 'What about the crew? Maybe the captain has lost his mind and is holding them hostage.' My imagination is working overtime. Mike is caught up by the drama too and we sit gripped, sipping our coffees and dipping into a shared apple crumble. Four times the vessel edges forwards, and four times it creeps backwards again. We watch, and wait for help to arrive. The harbour master? Police? Hostage negotiators? But no-one comes and eventually, feeling impotent and emotionally drained, there's no option but to go home.

As we make our way out, with our eyes unwillingly drawn towards the river, I mutter a little prayer to myself and cross my fingers. We're amongst the last customers to leave and although our waiter has probably had a long day, he still manages a friendly farewell. 'I hope you've had a good evening,' he says. 'Come back soon.' And then he laughs. 'You might see the sand dredger again.'

Making my peace

So far, the majority of this epic coastal walk has been new to me. We've completed the Dorset section, and the East Devon coast but this next stage from Paignton to Dartmouth takes in the area where I grew up and went to school.

Since my mother died twenty years ago, I've rarely been back to South Devon. And despite Claire's efforts with my Chagall-inspired painting, I still have many negative feelings about it. Memories of being trapped and biding my time until I could escape and get on with the grown-up part of my life. But maybe now that I've lived so much of that life, I will be more forgiving. Walking and being immersed in it might help – seeing, hearing, feeling and smelling things I would otherwise miss. And something else is different – this will be the first time that I've explored the area with Mike.

We base ourselves in Brixham and on the first day we set off along the coast towards Paignton. We walk for several miles through dense pine woods and as we make our way down a slope towards a tiny cove, we spot two shiny black heads bobbing in the sea. My first thought is that they're a pair of playful swimmers but I'm wrong. All those years I spent in Devon and this is the first time I've ever seen seals. It's a thrill to watch them as we sit on the pebbles sipping hot coffee from our flask. A man comes past with a corgi on a lead, and tells us that these seals are well-known locally. During the mating season the male has been known to nip unwary bathers.

In the evening, we linger on a bench above Brixham harbour, eating fabulously fresh fish. Mike praises the quality of the chips but I don't eat potatoes so I have a pickled egg instead. It's our first anniversary and we've brought our wedding poems to read to one another as the streetlights come on and a trawler prepares to creep out. In the background, a hill rises steeply up to the sky, higgledy-piggledy with uneven terraces and colourful cottages. I never liked this town when I was a teenager and came here to visit schoolfriends. It smelled of fish and seemed to have little going for it. But tonight, Mike says 'It's charming,' and I see it through his eyes.

He was charmed earlier today too, when we were standing under a huge viaduct as a steam train whistled and clattered above. I could see that it was picturesque, but I wasn't won over so easily. This was the line that I took to school every day.

'Shall we go on it tomorrow?' said Mike.

'Why would you want to do that?' I thought, remembering the infuriating trainspotters who would hang out of the windows with their cine cameras, and get in our way as we focused on making our escape from school. But I want him to enjoy his holiday so the next morning we park in Paignton and queue at the ticket office.

'Two returns, please,' I say.

'That will be £31,' says the ticket clerk. 'The engine pulling your carriage this morning is 75014. She was built at Swindon in 1954.'

We're a bit early so I sit on the platform reading my book. Mike paces around impatiently before announcing excitedly,

'There's some shunting going on over there,' and disappearing off to watch.

Shortly afterwards we chuff out of the town in a chocolate and cream carriage named Sarah, and when I stick my head out of the window, gusts of coal smoke catch in my throat, triggering memories. We pass Goodrington Sands which brings back images of melting ice-cream, getting lost when I was three, and worried strangers looming over me. Then we pass my school and there are more memories – the thrill of first-year English books, the ancient RE teacher who couldn't keep order, being lovesick, bunsen burners, the thwack of hockey sticks against hockey balls on frosty mornings, and the dark thrilling corners at Christmas discos.

We enter a long tunnel. I must have been through this on hundreds of journeys but *this* time I think of watching The Railway Children with *my* children. Then the River Dart starts to flash through the trees, and eventually the town of Dartmouth comes into full view on the opposite bank. 'It's so pretty,' says my husband hanging out of the window taking photos. And I have to agree that it is.

A shock

I am now officially in love with the South West Coast Path. 'It's *definitely* one of the most rewarding things I've ever done,' I gush to anyone who will listen. And it *is* – every day so different and vivid. The start of the morning is often a bit scratchy especially if the first stretch includes a big hill. But it doesn't take long to loosen up and by the time we stop for coffee and cake with stunning views, I'm where I want to be. I watch the waves crashing as they have every few seconds for millions of years and feel connected to something that is infinitely bigger than me. It makes my worries seem comfortingly insignificant.

Yes – the South West Coast Path and I are getting on very well indeed. We've walked 170 miles hand in hand and I dream of it when we're apart. I long to be with it again.

It *can* play hard to get though, and the logistics are often complicated. We don't necessarily walk a straight route from A to B, then B to C the following day. It all depends on where we're based, public transport timetables, and our energy levels.

Our latest section is from Start Bay to Salcombe and this time the logistics are the most convoluted yet. The plan is to leave the car at B, walk from there to C, take a bus to our accommodation inland, and the next morning get two buses to A and walk back to B. I was proud when I came up with this solution as it's become a point of principle to avoid using taxis unless absolutely unavoidable. Public transport is full of local characters and makes us feel more connected to the area.

We spend the night before our walk in Brixham again, and as we set off in the car the next morning, I feel a familiar glow of wellbeing at the prospect of pacing along for hours beside the sea. I do not know that this is the day when my dewy-eyed love affair will turn nasty. I do not know that this is the day when I will see a side of the Path that I do not like one little bit.

By mid-morning we're in the car park at Hallsands, and up on the cliffs we stop to read an information board. This was once a close-knit village that relied for survival on its fishing boats. But during the early years of the twentieth century the seabed was dredged and tons of shingle were taken away to be used in the construction of Plymouth Docks. Villagers expressed alarm at this loss of the natural defences but their concerns were ignored and the local press labelled them *moaners*.

In 1912 a wild storm swept the entire village into the waves. Miraculously no-one was killed but the community was destroyed forever.

Sobered by the sad story and the power of nature we carry on past cattle who chew and stare at us, and at Start Point lighthouse we agree that this would be a good time to bring out the coffee and the ginger cake. But as we perch on some steep rocks that slope down to more precipitous rocks and the sea, my stomach falls away and I have to move. Mike stays there, knees drawn up, enjoying the view and basking in the late summer sunshine.

We set off in the direction of Prawle Point and I still feel unsettled. The path is very high and alarmingly narrow with no hedge or fence to provide a safety net. I'd only have to twist my ankle and I'd be over the cliffs. I plod on with my walking poles, trying to breathe steadily and reminding myself that it's a dry day and my boots have good grip. I'm ashamed of my fear and keep my distance from Mike. I know that if I say anything to him my voice will come out squeaky and staccato, and I'll reveal my panic.

'Stay calm,' I say to myself over and over again. 'We must nearly be at the end of this stretch. Soon there will be a nice flat field or a friendly hedge to lean against.' But instead, the horror goes on and on. Time slows down and I'm on red alert, scanning every detail. Each tiny shift in the conditions releases a fresh heart-racing whoosh of adrenaline – a gust of wind, a slight irregularity in the path, turning my head sideways, looking down...and down. Where are the magpies when I need them? I've never longed to be a bird before but I am now pitifully aware of being a stumbling, earthbound human.

Then comes the final straw. The path is obstructed by enormous boulders – we have to clamber around them, and over them. They're a bit slimy and I don't trust my balance.

Enough.

I sink to the ground and cling to a jut of rock, alternately hyperventilating and sobbing. There is no way that I can go back and the prospect of going on is terrifying. Mike is a little way ahead but eventually sees that I've stopped and makes his way back, his face full of puzzled concern. 'Leave me here,' I whisper. 'I can't move.'

It takes energy that I can barely muster, to explain how I feel. He's astonished that I've been carrying this with me and it's completely outside his experience because he is fearless about physical danger. But he quickly absorbs what I'm saying and while he's towering over me wondering what to do, a young woman comes towards us. She's in hot pink shorts and she's running. She's having a wonderful day. Thirty seconds later another woman comes along – older, faster, and quite possibly her mother.

I feel nauseous, faint, and like my body is not big enough to contain the hammering panic it is busy producing. I don't know this term yet but I have a form of what mountain rescue teams call being *cragfast*. This is a new fear to add to my collection. One I wasn't aware I had although as I sit here shivering so unhappily, I have a flashback of a family holiday in Paris when I got a third of the way up the Eiffel Tower and froze. Will and Emma were teenagers. Solicitous and surprised, they led me down as I put my hands over my eyes and whimpered.

It takes an immense amount of patient cajoling to get me on the move again but in the end I manage it because I am sorry about placing Mike in this awkward situation. I hold onto his hand and edge along, feeling all the time that I am about to topple.

Eventually it is over. We are in woods approaching East Portlemouth and the firmness of the ground beneath my feet has never been more welcome. By the time we emerge onto a quiet road across the water from Salcombe it's nearly six o'clock and we've missed the last ferry. Our only option for reaching tonight's accommodation is a £30 taxi ride and we'll have to wait as the local minicab company is busy tonight. It's dark and drizzly and there's no pub or cafe so we sit for two hours at the side of the road. It hasn't been the best of days, and in the night I jerk awake several times as I tumble off a cliff.

The next morning I'm still jittery but due to our convoluted logistics we need to get a bus from Marlborough to Kingsbridge. And then another one to Strete from where we will walk along Slapton Sands to Hallsands and the car. Then we will drive home to Southampton.

I tell Mike I will do today's walk as it's mostly beach but I know that my love affair is over. I can't face the idea of future unfamiliar sections, any of which might ambush me. I am afraid of the Path and I am afraid of fear. I've faced it up in so many ways these past few years. But now it has won.

I didn't see this coming. It should not have come as a surprise that you can fall out of love so wholeheartedly. I should have already learned that. But it really does surprise me, and I am sad.

A windfall

Often when I wake up and check my phone, I find an urgent request for advice. Over the years I've rustled up rapid, early-morning responses on a range of topics – tax codes, vomiting boyfriends, job applications, mysterious boils on the feet, potential gas leaks, how to make coleslaw, the Tenancy Deposit Scheme, and What Am I For? These questions from my offspring keep me on my toes. They also help me to feel useful.

I'm quite good on employment, domestic and health questions but I'm not so strong on the existential ones. And it's not just my newly-adult children who are asking these questions because Mike has big changes on the horizon, too. For some time now, he's been speculating about retirement. It's all quite non-committal – almost playful. Possibly next year, maybe the one after. Definitely in three or four years.

Then without warning the pace accelerates. His university department is on a cost-cutting mission and the management makes Golden Goodbye offers to staff who are nearing the end of their career. They are, after all, much more expensive than the hungry, young postgrads who accept short-term, part-time contracts. There's a short window for response and we have long, searching conversations. Then suddenly within the course of a few weeks, it's all confirmed. He spends the quiet part of the summer tying up loose ends and in September he has a leaving party. The university caterers provide an excellent lunch and his colleagues speak warmly about him. When it's over we go home, make a cup of tea and sit in the garden.

The word *retire* derives from the French…*to withdraw to a place of safety and seclusion.*

I know that Mike feels cast adrift. He worries that he'll be bored without the intellectual stimulation of teaching and research. That he will become isolated after years of working alongside colleagues and being automatically included in social gatherings. He will have to construct his own routines and he will no longer have the office that provides a private space outside the home. He frets that he will no longer know who he is, and how he will answer when people ask what he does.

What will he be for?

On the plus side, there's the relief of stepping away from targets, aggressive management, restructuring, and endless marking. The nineteenth century American philosopher Henry David Thoreau dispensed many wise nuggets and I particularly like 'We should not calculate our wealth by how much we own but instead by how much free time we have.' It seems that within this economic model Mike is about to have a significant windfall, and I plan to follow within a year or two. The question remains of how to spend it.

Fortunately, he is blessed with curiosity and a wide range of interests. He plans to improve his French, to take up the piano again, to study the philosophy of science and the psychology of beliefs, to do more sailing, and to get to grips with a new camera. Less appealing are all the jobs in the house and garden that have been waiting for attention. But we're on the threshold of an important new phase and it deserves to be marked with something special. So we decide to put off the jobs that have been put off and have a short holiday.

Pass it on

It's the first Sunday of Mike's retirement, and we're on our way to spend five days in the Norfolk Broads. It's on my list because I'm curious to discover exactly what a Broad *is*. I asked several friends if they know and they all looked caught-out and said something along the lines of 'It's something to do with water, isn't it?' So I know I'm not alone in my ignorance. I'm hoping that when I see one it will all make sense. Mike is equally mystified, and happy to visit anywhere that means we can do some kayaking.

As we get deeper into Norfolk, I'm surprised to see that the names on the signposts are so unfamiliar. There are barely any that I recognise. But then perhaps it shouldn't come as such a surprise for this is an area that is tucked away in the rump of the country. You don't pass through on your way to somewhere else. You have to *intend* to go to this hidden watery wonderland.

We arrive at our accommodation which is a first-floor granny-flat attached to a cottage at Salhouse, a few miles outside Norwich. It has views across fields and is clean and well-equipped if a little stuck in *Diary of an Edwardian Lady* fussiness. Unfortunately, Mike's not feeling on top form so we have an early night and the next morning he wakes up with a sore throat so we abandon plans for cycling along a section of disused railway line. I'm sorry he's not feeling well but it's a treat to have a quiet day. I spend my time taking him hot drinks and reading about the meaning of life.

We can wonder what we're for and why we're here, and when I remind myself that I'm just one of 7.8 billion people on Earth I do indeed feel pretty small. But here's something *truly* mind-boggling. It's estimated that there are two trillion galaxies and if these were to be shared out amongst all the people alive right now then each one of us would get about 256 galaxies to ourselves. I could see this as a wondrous thing but instead it's so incomprehensible that it upsets me. It makes me feel infinitesimal and it's hard to believe it matters much whether I'm here or not.

In the film *Jackie*, the ex-First Lady talks to a priest just a few days after JFK's assassination. She's dazed by grief. 'What's the meaning of it all?' she asks. I find the priest's answer comfortingly straightforward. 'It takes a long time to realise it but the truth is that there are no answers. None.' And in *Pilgrim at Tinker Creek*, a meditation on the natural world, Annie Dillard quotes a woman who says with wise simplicity, 'Seem like we're just set down here, and don't nobody know why.'

You can search for the one true meaning as an essentialist or you can take the existentialist view that there are no answers. But however you deal with the *why*, the question remains of *how* to use the life we've been given. Even if you believe in an afterlife there's still an earthly lifetime to get through – the *why* can be consigned to the future but the *how* nags at the present. No moral code, religious or otherwise, comes with step-by-step instructions about careers, relationships, parenthood, retirement and all the other matters that clamour for clarity. Construct your own path. Lay the stones as best you can. Our paths are all so different.

As for how to make it all *matter*, then I like what existential psychiatrist Irvin Yalom calls *altruism*. There are the good deeds, for sure, and if someone has done you a kindness then pass it on to someone who needs it. Even if you don't know them. But Yalom's altruism is far broader than this and to understand it is to recognise that the ideas we share, the conversations we have, and the values we live by can influence others, often in ways that transcend generations. The more we learn and think, the richer the insights we have to share.

The next day Mike is feeling better so we drive through flat countryside to Wroxham which is on the River Bure and is otherwise known as the Capital of the Broads. We board a double-decker tour boat and before long we're discovering about the local area thanks to an informative commentary. First and most importantly I get to *see* a Broad and that makes all the difference to my understanding. It's a broad, shallow lake that opens onto any one of the seven rivers in the Broads National Park – the Bure, Thurne, Ant, Yare, Chet, Wensum, and Waveney. There are around sixty Broads and they were thought to be a natural feature until the 1950s when a young botanist named Joyce Lambert proposed a radical new theory. It hinged on the fact that East Norfolk was the most densely populated area in Europe in the twelfth century and because there was a big demand for fuel, there was extensive peat digging. This left enormous pits and when sea levels rose in the fourteenth century, the flooding created the lakes and marshes that we have now. Her ideas were greeted with scepticism at first but when she demonstrated that the edges of the Broads are vertical, it was widely accepted. If the Broads were a natural feature the banks would slope.

The following day we hire kayaks so we can immerse ourselves in the environment. It's only a short walk from our accommodation to Salhouse Broad and much of it is through woods where prehistoric ferns dominate, standing bright green against the weak sunshine. When we get to the lake we see a row of colourful kayaks drawn up on the small beach, and within a few minutes we're each sitting in one and floating on the water.

We paddle across the Broad and out into the open river. I'm wearing waterproofs but am already feeling warmly damp. I'm aware of the rough whorls of my fingerprints but it's not unpleasant and my main impression is of silence. It's there as a presence – the foreground to small or occasional sounds. Mostly there's just the gentle splash of our blades as we glide along. Then every now and again there's a hectic *flap, flap, flap* as a duck takes off or a Canada goose honks. The herons are still as ornaments and the swans stare, then turn away disdainfully as we pass.

Troops of weeping willows crowd down, dipping forwards as if to drink from the shady water, and untamed branches narrow the bends so that views are slow to reveal. But it's not all peace, and from time to time we hear the throb of a small Broads cruiser. I stop paddling as they pass. There are usually just a few people on board, and often a dog or two. The older people wave in a smooth downward motion like mechanical toys while small children flap energetically. I sit still after they go as the Mr Toad wash makes me bob me up and down. It's quite pleasant once I get used to it.

We've worked up an appetite and at last we round a sharp bend in the river at Horning and spot the Swan Inn, a black and white timbered pub where we've been told they do a good lunch. So we paddle towards the slipway, propel ourselves onto it and bump to a standstill. We leave small puddles as we walk to the bar, and my legs feel wobbly but the staff make us welcome and we place an order for fish and chips. The sweet potato variety for me. Then we take our drinks and find a vacant table in the garden.

We're feeling virtuous about our energetic morning and when our lunch appears we tuck in and enjoy the view down to the river where a couple of small Broads cruisers are moored. A family group goes past and we watch casually as they wander towards one of the boats. There's a thin, stooped lady with sparse white hair, and a frail-looking man, equally stooped. They look as though they've stepped out of the Elderly People road sign. They're with a woman who I assume is their daughter. She's wearing a casual grey top and trousers, and isn't moving fast but looks bouncy by comparison. The mother is first in line for the boat so the daughter provides an arm for support and then jumps on board herself. They're at the rear with the wheel. Next comes the old man who is near the front and grasps the chrome rail at the side of the boat. But before he can lift either of his feet off the grass, the daughter starts the engine and the back of the boat moves out. Mike shouts and we rush to the old man who is still holding onto the boat and is stretching further and further forwards. Time slows down. Another customer spots what's happening and helps Mike do a rugby tackle on the old man's legs while I grab his belt and pull as hard as I can. He's moving towards the horizontal and for a few long seconds it seems inevitable that we'll all end up in the river. Then at last, the daughter wakes up and steers the boat back in. The old man straightens up, looking distressed and I say 'I don't usually hold onto elderly gentlemen's belts' – which once out sounds thoroughly weird. Our fellow rescuer helps the old man onto the boat and within seconds, they're off. Apart from my belt-related comment no-one says anything. Nothing at all. It's only as we walk back to our seats that we exchange a few comments with the other customer – a *Phew that was a near miss* sort of thing. Then we sit down to finish our lunch.

On our way back to Salhouse we explore a couple of the Broads. It's like entering a house. You pass through a gap in the bank as if it were an open front door, then you go along a passageway and at the end the lake opens out like a large living room.

A few days later we're back home. I'm still wondering about those existential questions but I do think that Monty Python's *The Meaning of Life* is onto something. At the end, one of the characters is presented with an envelope which promises to reveal the secret. She tears it open and reads out the message inside –

It's nothing special. Try and be nice to people, avoid eating fat, read a good book every now and again, get some walking in, and try and live together in peace and harmony with people of all creeds and nations.

I agree with all of that but like I said we all have to lay our own path. So here's my current one. It's paved like this –

Walk in nature, eat salad, chat a lot, listen a lot, love, take help when you need it, be grateful for it, pass it on to anyone who needs it.

Savouring the Fall

It's the second week in October and I'm standing at a car rental desk at Boston Logan Airport. 'We *may not* have one of those cars after all,' says the reservations clerk glancing at my documents. 'You picked a *very small* vehicle. You'll need a bigger one for your trip.'

'That one's fine,' I say irritably. 'In England we have a small car. We *like* it.'

Mike nudges me even more irritably. 'We have a *normal-sized* car,' he says.

We rebuff three more rounds of upselling and eventually climb into our normal-sized/small American car and set off through Boston's maze of tunnels. The focus of our trip is the autumn foliage in New England but before that we're spending a couple of days on Cape Cod.

We've booked an AirBnB at Yarmouth which is one of the two oldest towns on the peninsula. It is, of course, named after Great Yarmouth in Norfolk which in turn gets *its* name because it's at the mouth of the River Yare. It seems disjointed to find a Yarmouth with no river to give it authenticity. But I clearly need a different mindset here as the town names leak the histories of the settlers and the homes they left behind. There's Braintree, Weymouth, Plymouth, Rochester, Falmouth, Taunton, Sandwich, Truro, Chatham – even small places like

Plympton and Wareham are represented. These English place names have simply been transposed and reveal nothing about the local topography or customs. Other names are unfamiliar but divulge more about themselves – Cranberry Bog, Old Meeting House Swamp, Buzzards Bay, Brickyard Creek, Flax Pond…

Then there are the ones that I stare at before cautiously attempting to work my mouth around them. These are the ones that give a true sense of place, the ones that are derived from the native American words, and have survived being trampled. There's Wequaquet Lake from the Wampanoag for *end of the land*, and Waquoit which means *place of light*. Mashpee is another name that strikes me as curious and it turns out to be the official home of what remains of the Mashpee Wampanoag tribe. Back in 1620 their ancestors helped the Pilgrims to survive before gradually losing their lands to the English colonisers. All of these familiar and unfamiliar names provide a haphazard commentary on this place of contrasts – tamed and wild, light and dark, gain and loss.

If the peninsula is likened to a human arm curling around Cape Cod Bay, then Yarmouth is somewhere between the shoulder and the elbow. Our host Susan is a retired professor and makes us welcome. She spent childhood summers here and her current house was once a parsonage with some parts dating from the 1700's. We go up the steps onto a white painted veranda, and into our room which has pale wicker furniture and airy paintings of beaches and the ocean. There's a huge bathroom with a freestanding tub in the middle. Later, Susan invites us into her kitchen for coffee and local tips. We talk about this and that, and American politics – and agree on many things.

Next day we explore the wide Cape beaches. We park at Marconi Beach and make our way down a great flight of wooden steps edged by tufty marram grass and thin palisade fencing, parts of which are overwhelmed by sand drifts. We've missed the summer bathers, skimboarders, boogie boarders and kite surfers. And we've also missed any chance of spotting dolphins, whales or the great white sharks who come here in pursuit of gray seals. Instead, we let the autumn winds blow us about, feel the fine sand sift past our bare toes, and stare out at the vast, slatey Atlantic.

We drive through charming towns with clapboard churches and perfectly proportioned spires. The one in Chatham has hundreds of Halloween pumpkins outside, in higgledy-piggledly piles. The sky is sapphire, the fruits are deep orange and the building is pure white. It's a seductive image. And then there's Provincetown. At the curled fingertips of the peninsula, it's where the Mayflower landed in 1620. But the museum is closed today. So instead we explore the modern character of this small town. It's a popular resort with the LGBT+ community and the main street is full of old wooden buildings wearing rainbow flags. I lick my ice cream and a drag queen winks at me, all tight jeans, bangles and totteringly-high block heels.

On Friday morning we have a goodbye coffee with Susan and set off for Ashland in New Hampshire. Its proximity to the White Mountains and Squam Lakes makes it popular with tourists but we're out of season and the town is quiet. Our accommodation is in an 'old' building and the artist-owners have filled it with cheerful cushions, paintings and pottery. They've also provided art materials, a yoga mat and a smart coffee machine.

On Saturday we drive to the nearby town of Meredith for the highlight of our holiday – a four-hour Fall Foliage Excursion on the heritage Winnipesaukee Scenic Railroad. We collect our tickets from inside a reverently restored 1890 baggage car and then mill around with the other passengers.

Our snowy-haired conductor is in the yard, attempting to stride around but being waylaid by one enthusiastic passenger after another. He answers questions, makes small talk, and nods a lot. He's clearly loving it. His black peaked cap with a gold badge confirms his status as a railroad official, and his white double-breasted jacket is pristine. He hovers genially somewhere between 1890 and a 1940s Hollywood movie.

When we board the train, we notice with a hint of envy that some passengers are travelling in President's Class. They're looking pleased with themselves, stretching out on spacious couches while we're in Coach Class with young families and grandparents in a noisy chaos of rucksacks and juice cartons. But our attention soon shifts outside as we pass Lake Waukewan with its houses dotted along the shore and little wooden pontoons that reach out into the silent water.

The conifers here stand tall and straight. They are sober and steadfastly green in the shady gloom but across the lake and on the distant mountains it couldn't be more different. Their deciduous neighbours are having a party. They're flaunting their reds, oranges and yellows in an awesome display. I grope for words and then get carried away with the sensuousness of it all – peach, ginger, strawberry ice cream, acid yellow, lime, rust, gold, olive, pumpkin, tomato, sunshine, cherry, terracotta, auburn, saffron, mustard, red hot chilli…

We clatter through the countryside with occasional sightings of local industry. There's a mill pond and then the Rochester Shoe Tree factory appears next to the line, tucked away in the forest like a Hansel and Gretel house. It has four pink-framed windows and a steeply pitched roof. Outside are massive piles of cedar wood, no doubt beautifully fragrant. Later there's a deer farm, and at Glove Hollow Tree Farm we see thousands of Christmas trees, thriving on the flat grassland at the foot of the mountains.

By one o'clock we're in Plymouth where a buffet lunch has been laid on at a restaurant in a former wood mill. I sit with Mike on my left and a couple of American women to my right. They're engrossed in conversation so I turn to an older man across the table. 'Good foliage but not spectacular,' he states flatly and then applies full concentration to his turkey kebab.

After a bit, the woman on my right puts down her fork and turns to me, all wide-eyed attention. 'So, what's *your* total, then?' she asks.

'It's my first trip here,' I say. 'I'm enjoying it very much.' She shakes her head. This is clearly not the right answer and as she looks towards Mike, I think that perhaps she's asking about husbands. 'Two?' I say tentatively.

She's not impressed. 'Mine's thirty-eight,' she says proudly.

I can't think what to say.

She gestures to the woman on her right. 'My friend and I... We always travel together. Our last trip, we did Switzerland and Germany. Before that it was Peru and Bolivia.'

I attempt a quick tally of the countries I've visited. 'I don't know,' I say limply.

She looks *deeply* disappointed and turns away.

Later, on the train ride back I add them up but I can't equal her total – even by splitting the UK into Wales, Scotland and Northern Ireland. And not even by including England where I've lived all of my life.

We don't have plans for the evening but when our host sees us coming back, he sticks his head out of the window and recommends the local microbrewery. It was set up a few years ago by a retired hobbyist. He says it's getting great reviews and Mike loves a good pint so we decide to give it a try. By now it's completely dark and we wander along unlit, deserted side streets lined with widely-spaced houses until all evidence of human habitation peters out and a sign directs us round the back of a factory unit. There, we find a couple of chunky trucks and a small wooden building, and as I stand in the doorway peering through the foggy glass, I see some shadowy figures moving around inside. I've no idea what to expect so I push Mike in first.

Half a dozen men are sitting at the bar, hunched over their beer glasses. They're in jeans and checked shirts and as we enter, they stop talking and stare. We probably look like we've stumbled in by mistake. There's a pause. Then one of the men steps forward. He has glasses, dark eyebrows and a spectacular white handlebar moustache. 'Welcome to my brewery!' he says. And that's the start of a terrific evening.

We're the only non-locals. There are seats at the bar, and a couple of tables but everyone's so chatty that we never get to sit down. Thirty minutes later and Mike's on his second pint. 'This guy knows what he's doing,' he whispers. 'It's like English bitter but tangy and smoky. Quite distinct.'

Tammy's helping out behind the bar while her husband has a drink. It's a proper community enterprise but for now she and

I are the only women. Then a young couple come in. They're locals too. I get into conversation with the woman, while Mike talks to her husband. It's one of those rapid-fire discussions where you know time is limited and there's a lot to share. She teaches physics at a local high school and tells me how Trump's election divided people. 'It makes it really hard when I go to see my family in Florida. Some of them voted for him.'

'We have a camper van,' she continues. 'Every summer we put the dogs in it, and then we just drive off and explore. Last year we ended up in Kentucky. It was interesting to talk to people and find out about their lives. So different from ours. I tell my pupils…you must travel. It's the best way to understand.'

Conversations like this are unexpected gifts. Never mind the countries – I'll collect these instead.

Being here

This holiday in America includes a second treat. The last time I did an overnight train journey was at the age of thirteen on the London to Glasgow sleeper, and ever since I've longed to recapture the romance of falling asleep to the rhythm of wheels, and the magic of waking up in the dawn light to a new landscape. And I *particularly* want to do it in this country that I know mostly through the movies.

There are dozens of routes to choose from and I could easily settle for those that take in New Orleans, Orlando or San Francisco. But in the end, I decide on the service that connects Washington DC and Chicago. These are cities that Mike and I are both keen to visit and although the journey is the point of this treat it would be a shame to waste the opportunities at either end. I book the tickets several months ahead and note that we will be leaving Washington DC at four on a Friday afternoon and arriving in Chicago at nine the following morning, fresh for a weekend of exploring.

Everything is going well but then a couple of weeks before we are due to leave, I fall ill. For a week I sleep almost continuously and as I emerge from this phase I notice a rash on my right ankle. It itches like crazy and then it spreads to my leg. Before long there are *hundreds* of hillocks with new ones erupting as I watch. They are everywhere except on my face and the soles of my feet. By now, it is just three days until our flight and my body has been hijacked by a John Wyndham plot.

I sit in front of my GP, tearful and dramatic as I explain my dilemma. He shifts his glasses on and off as he peers at my spots. He seems impressed. 'I'm pretty sure you've got a staphylococcal infection,' he says, 'but we'll take a swab and send it off, just to confirm.' He adds that a ten-day course of penicillin will probably clear it up and he can't see any reason to abandon the holiday. He turns out to be right.

I had everything planned. I felt I had it so well under control and yet it nearly didn't happen. This time I escape with a relatively trivial complaint but growing older brings with it the inevitable recognition that far from getting better at controlling our lives, we're not actually in control at all.

A couple of years ago when one of my most beloved friends was dying from motor neurone disease we gathered our families together. My four adult children and her three – our families entwined for so many years and now Nicky in a wheelchair. We exchanged stories and when Will mentioned that he was planning a trip to Budapest, Nicky said, 'I'd love to have gone there.' I was struck by the way she said it. Wistful but also accepting the inevitability that she would never go.

Nearing my sixtieth birthday is also a jolt. It's the first decadal birthday when you can be almost sure that you are over half-way through your life. It's possible to hold onto a *tiny* bit of doubt as Jeanne Calment was 122 when she died in France in 1997. But that was *one* person. The next oldest documented case didn't quite make it to 120.

I've dreamed of doing this train journey for so long. I'd better make the most of it.

After leaving New Hampshire we spend a few hectic days in New York and then have thirty-six hours in Washington. We picnic on the grass outside the Capitol Building. I keep expecting to be moved on but we're left to munch our hummus wraps and to watch the Government workers strolling in the sunshine. Afterwards we walk up the National Mall and then alongside the Memorial Wall, polished black granite inscribed with over 58,000 names of US servicemen and servicewomen who lost their lives or went missing in the Vietnam War. The scale is astonishing. In contrast, the White House looks much smaller than I expected and there's a crowd of young black men outside. They're all wearing red baseball caps with Trump's slogan – Make America Great Again.

There are many more monuments to see, and at the end of the afternoon we make our way across the Potomac River to a modern apartment in a tall block. This time our Airbnb host is a sharp young woman who works in Government. She tells us stories of life on *the Hill* and clearly has had lots of practice at rolling her eyes. They do a complete circuit when she talks about the President.

Next morning, it's a short subway ride to the Arlington National Cemetery. JFK visited here for Veterans Day commemorations in 1963 and as he stood on the peaceful hillside looking across to the Washington Monument, the US Capitol and the Lincoln Memorial, he told a park ranger 'I could stay here forever.' Eleven days later he was dead. We stand next to his grave.

Mid-afternoon we make our way to Union Station and are there in good time for our train. I enjoy the imposing building which dates back to a Golden Age when railroad companies wanted their customers to feel special, and as we stand patiently in a long queue, the man in front steps on my toes. When the gate finally opens, we all press forward onto the platform and there waiting for us is our huge, metal-clad Superliner train.

Whenever I travel, I spend a lot of time wondering what it will be like to come back. Perhaps with someone else. What will I think then? Will I be suffused with bliss? Possibly. But most probably I will be thinking about the next trip. Is this an attempt to make happiness feel permanent? To take the pleasure of the current moment into the future and to keep hold of it? It's a common foible and in *The Art of Travel* Alain de Botton writes that it doesn't matter how rich and enjoyable an experience is, it's somehow ruined because we bring ourselves along on the ride. Now as we walk along the platform, I remind myself that this moment – this *actual* moment – is the one I've looked forward to for many months. I am exactly where I want to be.

It's a long train and eventually we find our carriage and are greeted by a uniformed steward. He's diffident and polite and he looks tired. His name is Bill and he directs us to our compartment on the upper deck, where we have a big window and two generous seats facing one another. We kick off our shoes and at 4.05pm the train pulls out. We have 780 miles to travel before we reach Chicago. On the way we will pass through Maryland, West Virginia, Pennsylvania, Ohio, Indiana and finally Illinois. I watch through the window as the light slowly fades. By 6.30 it's dark.

Dinner is the main event of the evening and Bill calls us through to the dining car. With images cast by Hitchcock in *The Lady Vanishes*, I'd imagined waiter service, linen tablecloths and menu choices, but it's not like that at all. Amtrak has started serving pre-packed meals as part of a cost-cutting drive. They've been losing business to the airlines for years. The food is pleasant enough – Asian noodle bowls with a brownie to follow – and there's a choice of wine, beer and soft drinks. But in the end the food doesn't matter as much as I thought it would, because quite simply, I *love* being on the train.

We nod and smile tentatively at the cheery man who is sitting alone at the opposite table. We're all careful to be restrained, mindful of one another's privacy. But eventually he is no longer able to contain himself. He leans across the aisle and confides that lots of people are unhappy about this new scheme. 'If enough of us ring and complain,' he says, 'they might bring back the old service.'

We have a bit more neighbourly, neck-craning interaction and then Mike points at his bottle of wine. 'Come and join us. You can share this,' he says. Seconds later our companion is seated at our table – round glasses, twinkly eyes, a shiny round face, and a round head with just a little white hair to fence it in. We all introduce ourselves. He's another Bill and is delighted to discover that we're from England. He tells us that his family emigrated from Frome in the 1700s and that he is a pastor in a Congregationalist church. But he's not here to evangelise. Instead, he glances around cautiously and lowers his voice conspiratorially. He says that he and many other liberal-minded pastors are deeply concerned about the potential erosion of rights under the current administration. They worry that recent progress is under threat, and that gay marriage, for example, could be banned in some states. He talks and he listens. The train rattles along and when all the wine is drunk and the other passengers have disappeared, we bid him a fond goodnight.

Steward Bill has been busy while we've been away and has reconfigured our compartment, transforming the seats into bunk beds. I take a shower in a compact bathroom on the lower deck. The water is hot and there's a pile of fluffy, white towels.

I'm much shorter than Mike so I volunteer to take the top bunk and once I'm up there I have no choice but to settle down for the night. There's not enough space to sit up. I lie in the dark – warm and comfortable, loving the horn which sounds at every crossing. And as I'm drifting off, another train snakes past, its fleeting whoosh so different from our steady, comforting rattle. It's raining and I imagine all the lonely people we are passing, seated in Hopperesque diners. I think, too, of Marilyn Monroe's illicit train party in *Some Like it Hot*. When I wake up to go to the loo, I wriggle down the bunk to the ladder like an earthworm.

We're woken by Steward Bill's gentle tones over the PA system. 'Good morning, ladies and gentlemen. The time is 7.45. Please make your way to the dining car for breakfast.' Shortly after, we're back at our table with Pastor Bill and breakfast which is fresh fruit, yogurt, and a granola bar. We pass massive stretches of golden wheat with huge irrigation machines straddling the fields. It's impossible not to think of crop duster planes and Cary Grant's impeccable grey suit.

Bill tells us that he is on his way to visit an old college friend who is sinking into dementia. 'If you want to see him,' the friend's wife said, 'you'd better do it soon.'

As we swap stories, there's an announcement. The train is running late because we've been stuck behind a slow freight train for much of the night. 'We appreciate your patience,' says Steward Bill apologetically. We settle down in the observation car, feet stretched out, sipping coffee and watching Indiana flash past. It has floor to ceiling windows and never have I been so delighted by a train delay.

Eventually Lake Michigan comes into view and at Chicago Union station we say farewell to the two Bills. The ride has taken twenty hours. We could have flown in a tenth of the time. I'm so glad we didn't.

2018

Extra time

I'm enjoying life at the moment. Compared with past turbulent years it's heaven to have fewer things to worry about. That's not to say I'm ready to thumb my nose at any magpies yet or to walk under ladders but I *am* wholeheartedly grateful for this stage.

Which is why it's particularly annoying that time seems to whizz by. I might have chosen to fast-track my childhood if I could but feel different about where I am now. I'd be content to linger longer. *Very* content. Instead, what happens? These happier years are simply *flashing* past.

Most people report that time seems to go faster as they get older and the most convincing explanation I've come across is that as we age, we're more inclined to follow routines and to repeat things we've already done. A normal day at home may be perfectly pleasant but because it's safe and predictable then nothing stands out. When we look back on it, there are few if any memories to mark that time and so in retrospect it seems to have passed quickly. On the other hand, when we step outside our usual experience, we automatically become alert in order to keep ourselves safe. With plenty of information to process, things seem vivid and so they're more likely to make an impression. The time may seem to pass quickly in the moment especially if we're absorbed but when we look *back* on that period of time, the more memories there are to draw on, the longer it appears to have lasted.

Objectively there's nothing I can do to slow time down but maybe – just maybe – with snatches of novelty here and there it will *feel* longer in retrospect. I tried walking a different route to the shops this week. It took me along a shady lane past a school that I didn't know existed, and when I got to the greengrocery stall, I bought some enoki mushrooms, which I've never done before. I can still remember that trip but the one the previous week was indistinguishable from countless other humdrum errands.

I hadn't thought of my list in this way before but it *is* largely about having new experiences. And the latest has been a trip to St Petersburg. I've long been fascinated by the romance and otherness of Russia and as it turns out it's lucky I went when I did because we all know what happened a few years later in 2022.

Our visit is during the White Nights in June when it never gets fully dark. But we don't get off to a great start. Late in the afternoon, we stand outside our apartment with the rain pouring and Mike informs me that this is the area where Raskolnikov committed the grisly murder in *Crime and Punishment*. A century and a half may have passed since then but it still feels edgy. Our phones aren't working and we can't figure out how to get into our block so we tentatively ring a few doorbells and Mike flexes his basic Russian.

Several people shout back, sounding angry and then eventually someone gives a big sigh and buzzes us in. Our flat is a single room in the basement and comes without frills. The double sheet is more like a tablecloth and doesn't quite cover the bed. But it's just a base from which to explore and we're happy to have somewhere that is clean, convenient and cheap in a city awash with expensive tourist hotels.

It was three centuries ago that Peter the Great chose the Neva Delta as the location for his dream city – the one that would open up trade routes and be the *window on Europe* in his quest to modernise Russia. But this was inhospitable, mosquito-infested swampland and underneath today's grand pavements lie the bones of an estimated 30,000 serfs and Swedish prisoners of war who perished as they laboured with bare hands to build the city. Peter's ambition was unstoppable and when faced with a shortage of building materials he simply imposed a ban on using stone for construction anywhere else in Russia. And he decreed that all visitors to the area, whether on a ship or pushing a handcart, must bring a contribution of stones. Fortunately, although we had to go through some convoluted bureaucracy in order to get our visas, we were not asked to bring any rubble.

This is a place where unimaginable wealth has existed side by side with extreme poverty and there are numerous jaw-dropping buildings around the city. It has been devastated by floods and fire, witnessed countless assassinations and executions, and its streets have run with blood as protests have turned violent. Meanwhile spies and counter agents have lingered in the shadows.

On our first full day of sightseeing, we decide to take a trip out to the Peterhof complex of palaces. It's twenty-five kilometres outside the city and the quickest way is by hydrofoil. We pass along the River Neva slowly at first, taking in the ornate buildings that line the banks in primrose yellow, mint green and birthday cake pink. But as we leave these behind, the hydrofoil has a powerful burst of acceleration and we thrash across the Gulf of Finland, bumping up and down as brown, foamy sea crashes against the windows.

When we arrive, we join the tourist crocodile and quickly realise that everything is on such a vast scale that we have no idea where to start. There is no obvious guidance so we wander through the gardens and try to orient ourselves amidst the bewildering assortment of palaces and fountains. Peter got his inspiration from Versailles and, never prepared to be outdone, he commanded his designer to come up with something that was more impressive. Inside the Grand Palace I'm so dazzled by the sheer amount of crystal and gilt that I reach for my sunglasses.

When it was completed, St Petersburg became the Russian capital and home to a succession of ostentatious rulers. Empress Anna kept a different horse for every day of the year and her lover Count Biron had two hundred jewel-studded saddles. Then there was the Empress Elizabeth who spent most of her time in military uniform but still felt the need for several thousand pairs of shoes. She lost around four thousand dresses in a fire and after her death a further fifteen thousand were discovered. She was popular as she pledged not to execute anyone during her reign. Peter, by contrast, found public executions thoroughly entertaining.

And it's here at Peterhof that we meet another ruler who shaped the city. Catherine the Great was a Prussian princess who married Peter the Great's grandson. But he was generally agreed to be cruel and weak, and six months after he became Tsar Peter III, she led a palace coup that forced him to abdicate. He was later assassinated – probably by Catherine's lover – and she ruled Russia for the next thirty-four years.

At the end of our visit we stand on a terrace looking out over the enormous water feature that cascades down from the Grand Palace. It's comprised of sixty-four individual fountains, dozens of bronze ornaments and a huge gilded statue. It's a hot day and we enjoy the cool mist and the tiny glinting rainbows.

On Saturday morning we head for the centre of the city, and the Hermitage Museum. This includes the Winter Palace which has nearly two thousand windows. It houses the largest collection of paintings in the world and was started by Catherine the Great. But although she amassed treasures her motivation was not a love of art. 'I am a glutton,' she said and took particular delight in outbidding Frederick the Great of Prussia, who was hobbled by debt after the Seven Years' War. There are about three million items here. We have half a day…

As we move through the museum, I begin to pick out Catherine from amongst the many other portraits…ruddy cheeks…imperious…sturdy…usually seated on a horse…She hated to be outshone by the ladies at her court, so she ordered them to shave their heads and then sent poor-quality black wigs for them to wear.

There's so much here that I have to be glad for what I do see and not regret what I miss. A favourite moment is when I stand next to Catherine's golden state sleigh and look out of the window onto the Neva. I imagine it frozen.

On Sunday morning we go to the State Museum of the Political History of Russia and stand by a portrait of the final tsar, Nicholas II. He looks regal in his military uniform but it's impossible to ignore the great marks in the painting where it was slashed with bayonets on the night he was captured by Bolsheviks. In this building we also see the room where Lenin worked on essays and speeches in the months leading up to the storming of the Winter Palace. Outside the window is the balcony from where he addressed the crowds of workers and soldiers. The museum is quiet during our visit and there's plenty of time to take in the dusty, bookish atmosphere of this room that changed the world.

In the evening, we spend an interesting few hours hopping on and off the Metro. St Petersburg has the deepest subway in the world thanks to problematic geology, and is well worth a visit for its own sake. It was opened during the Soviet era and many of the stations have huge chandeliers, marble columns, statues, and mosaics. We see tributes to Lenin, Pushkin, Russian sport, and Soviet industry.

When we get back to the UK, I realise that neither of us bought a souvenir. Not even a fridge magnet. It didn't occur to us. We squeezed a lot into the four days and as always when you're having fun, they passed all too quickly. But they were packed with things that I found new and surprising and so what we *do* have are plenty of time-decelerating memories. And these souvenirs come with many advantages – they don't need dusting, they don't take up space, and I will never have to guiltily bag them up and take them to a charity shop.

Challenging the magpies

It's mid-afternoon on a winter Monday and we're walking home after a relaxing lunch beside the fire in a local pub. There's a direct route that takes us through the woods to the back of our house and it's pleasantly frosty. 'We really *are* living a charmed life at the moment, aren't we,' says Mike, full of good cheer and a pint or two.

'*Ssshhh!*' I cry, looking around for any magpies who might be listening. '*Don't* say that!'

'Are you having a superstitious moment?' he asks. And he smiles. Because he can. He can't hear a clenched maternal voice saying –

> *Don't tempt fate.*
>
> *Don't tempt fate.*
>
> *Don't ever, ever tempt fate.*

It's now more than five years since we met and I remember how I could see such potential happiness with this interesting man but I was scared to enjoy it. We'd only been together a few months when he took the plunge and invited me to join him at his brother's wedding in South Africa. That was eight months away and so it was an act of faith for him to ask and for me to accept. 'If we stay together till December and your brother's wedding…' I'd say only half joking, whenever the subject of our joint future came up. Once Cape Town became a happy memory, I substituted Glastonbury as a milepost. That came and went. New events were inserted into the boilerplate text as necessary, until the words *our wedding* hung in the air and my reticence seemed silly.

I might have carried on indefinitely rationing joy, saluting magpies and hoping for the best. But a couple of things have shifted. The first is that when you get close to someone new you come up against different ways of dealing with life and it forces you to see yourself in sharper focus. I thought it inevitable that anyone who has suffered loss – and by middle age that surely applies to most of us – will be haunted by the fragility of life. But despite having lost one wife to cancer, Mike does *not* automatically expect things to go wrong. He is pragmatic and steady and wants to make the best of what he has right now.

The second has been reading Brené Brown's *Daring Greatly*. She writes about how being happy can make you vulnerable because you fear losing it. She describes a pattern of behaviour that she calls 'foreboding joy' and I recognise it only too well – constantly preparing for the worst when things are at their best. That way disappointment cannot take you by surprise. I was three when I learned to fear disappointment. My father would write to my mother to say he'd be coming for the weekend. But we had no phone, and there was no indication of exactly when he'd be turning up so my mother would get some steak for him, and then on Saturday afternoon we'd set off optimistically along the grass verge at the side of the road – out into the countryside, eyes peeled for his old black Jaguar coming over the horizon. More often than not, we came back alone, and my mother would say, 'Don't be disappointed, dear.' Then I would cry, soaked through with *her* disappointment and feelings of abandonment. I could never be sure that the heaving sobs would stop. They seemed to have a life of their own. They scared me, and so did that word, disappointment.

'Challenge it,' says Brené Brown. 'Face the fear. Allow yourself to feel vulnerable.'

I'll try.

There *are* plenty of good things happening at the moment. Mike is not missing work anything like as much as he thought he would, and as I get nearer to my sixtieth birthday there is a flurry of treats. Mostly bigger ones that have had to hang back while I work out what I want from them. And one of the few remaining treats is a river cruise. I've never been happy on the sea with its vast emptiness and sickening swell but I enjoy being on water and dream of sitting at a picture window watching the riverbank passing by.

I was tempted by cruises along the Rhône or through Portugal's Douro Valley. But even the shortest of these at seven nights, would make a crater in our holiday budget so I kept postponing the decision. Then I came across a four-day Christmas market cruise on the Rhine – it was the right length and price, so I booked. And so here we are, arriving in Cologne on a December evening to join our brand-new ship, all glossy wood, gleaming brass, and thick carpets. I have to confess that I am somewhat relieved to discover that we've arrived too late for the welcome cocktail party.

Early next morning we're on the move. We're travelling downriver to Rüdesheim and following an afternoon there, the ship will cruise slowly back over several days making stops at Koblenz and Bonn before a final evening in Cologne. We're on the middle deck and our cabin has picture windows. It's seasonally frosty outside but we're warm in our comfy chairs, reading, drinking coffee and watching the great muddy river swirl past.

This is every bit as delightful as I'd hoped it would be. There are many romantic castles and fortresses on the cliffs along the forty miles of Gorge and some have lain in picturesque ruins since the Thirty Years War. In the cold winter light, the sky is a watercolour wash of silver and pewter, and the steep terraced vineyards are khaki.

This part of the Rhine is rich in folklore and when we reach the narrowest section, an announcement alerts us to the bronze Lorelei statue on the rocks. According to legend she was a beautiful local maiden who drowned after an unhappy love affair and is now a mermaid. She spends her days singing across the water to lure boatmen to their death.

I know that folklore and its cousin, superstition, have been passed from generation to generation to help people contend with forces that are largely outside their control. But as a citizen of a more rational age, I feel I should be able to come up with something better – something more considered than the magpies and the stranglehold of foreboding joy. And it's sobering to admit that all the effort I put into trying to allay bad luck only keeps the fear alive and fuels the insecurity. It's counterintuitive but fits with the Backwards Law proposed by the philosopher Alan Watts. He observed that in many areas of life, the harder, we try, the less successful we are.

Having this new concept of foreboding joy means that I can at least *sometimes* recognise what was previously invisible. And when I do this, I can *sometimes* trap it and prevent it causing further damage. The key to trapping it is to remind myself that I am feeling wholeheartedly happy – and that cannot harm me. It takes practice.

It's been a sublime morning and after lunch on board, we set off to explore the small town of Rüdesheim. The narrow medieval streets are thronged today as people wander past the Christmas market stalls. There are quantities of musical boxes, wooden nutcrackers and every kind of Christmas decoration, but we avoid temptation as we already have too much *stuff* after merging our households. Instead, we choose a traditional stollen, wrapped in waxed white paper, spiced and heavy with dried fruit and marzipan.

The next morning in Koblenz, the highpoint of our tour is the Basilica of St Castor with its two Romanesque towers and painted starry ceilings. There are around eighteen hundred basilicas worldwide but I've never known what distinguishes them from other kinds of churches. Today I resolve to plug this gap in my knowledge and by the time we leave, I know that it is a Catholic church of special importance and that the distinction can only be conferred by a Pope. This one was promoted to basilica status by Pope John Paul II in 1991. One of the unique features of a basilica is the presence of an umbraculum – a large silk umbrella, striped in papal red and gold – which is kept in a conspicuous position beside the altar. It's there to symbolise the connection between the basilica and the Vatican and is only opened when the Pope pays a visit. I'm not sure what my mother would have to say about *that*. Opening an umbrella indoors...

Later, we have our third dinner on board – the food is excellent and the staff are charming. The only thing I don't enjoy are the forced conversations with other passengers. We never seem to get beyond establishing where people come from, where they've been on previous cruises, and what they bought in the market today. It reminds me how easy it is to feel alone in a crowd. We excuse ourselves early and return to the blissful peace of our cabin where we fall asleep with the curtains open and the riverbank gliding past.

In the morning we wake up to snowfall in Bonn and after breakfast we crunch along the elegant, spacious streets to the sound of Sunday church bells. It's bitterly cold and I'm glad to swathe my face in the lambswool shawl I bought in Arles. We explore the city centre which was devastated by heavy bombing in the war and has been rebuilt in keeping with the medieval layout. One of the few buildings not to have been damaged is Beethoven's birthplace, a solid house, painted salmon pink with dark green doors and window shutters. We pass the Minster and although it's closed for major repairs, I see that it's a basilica, and brimming with yesterday's enlightenment find myself worrying about their umbraculum and hoping they've put it somewhere safe during the renovations.

From the Minster it's just a short distance to the Christmas market and the first thing we see is Beethoven standing on a plinth, frowning across the square and incongruous in front of a Ferris wheel. There are dozens of stalls serving sausages, potato pancakes, pizza, roasted chestnuts, gingerbread, and glühwein. But nothing tempts us. Although the food on the ship is very good, we're not used to fancy breakfasts day after day. So we go into a cafe on the edge of the market and I order some fresh peppermint tea.

After the lightest of lunches we retreat to our cabin for this final part of the journey. We arrive in Cologne as it's getting dark and it's a short amble along the riverbank to the Gothic cathedral. It may be the country's most visited landmark but it is *not,* I note, a basilica. The largest of the city's seven Christmas markets is here, in the shadow of this great building and it's on a completely different scale from those we've seen before. There's a giant tree lit up with a canopy of 50,000 lights. And nearby is a stage where a grey-haired rock band plays carols. It's undeniably cheesy but the atmosphere is family-oriented and festive. We nibble at a shared slice of hot cherry strudel and Mike drinks mulled wine. I'm a lightweight with a hibiscus-infused kinderpunsch. This is German hygge and I thumb my nose at the foreboding that tries to press in. Once again, I remind myself that being happy cannot harm me. If a plane were to fall out of the sky and squash my loved ones it would not be my happiness that had caused it.

Nor would it be that magpie I accidentally snubbed last week.

Standing on shoulders

Like most inquisitive cooks I own a stack of cookery books but while I enjoy trying new recipes, it's not always easy to remember which ones are worth making again and where they came from. And so, several decades ago I started typing up those that work, together with a few words about their origin and when I first made them. I keep these in a loose-leaf file and although not the original intention, it has grown into a family memory book. There's the chocolate cheesecake that I made for Henry's christening, Will's favourite lemon ice-cream and the Cranks red bean and aubergine stew that I've been making for thirty years. At the beginning of a recipe for baked vanilla plums, I note that I first made them when my late friend Nicky gave me a bag of fruit from her garden. I miss her, and reading the recipe conjures up instant memories of her affectionate teasing and effortless elegance. My blurb also mentions that this recipe was a good way of using up the fruit from our own plum tree. 'Did we have a plum tree?' I ask myself. I have no recollection of that at all so I ask Emma and she confirms that we did.

The file is unintentionally entertaining because I type quickly and Word inserts random acts of auto-completion. So the pages are peppered with ridiculous instructions such as *Add one teaspoon of ground finger* to a spiced loaf cake, and *Serve the hummus in a pretty owl*. One recipe instructs me to pour the lovely brownie mixture that I've just made into the *bin*, and the ingredients for one of my favourite soup recipes include 750ml of boiling *watercress*. *Cooking* a completed dish for ten minutes results in tough food when you were really supposed to cool it for ten minutes.

I learned to cook with Delia by my side, and later it was Nigella who inspired with her playful recipes, and Gary Rhodes who added solid techniques and a touch of sophistication. These days I'm more likely to turn to Yotam Ottolenghi or Meera Sodha but I've always been curious about Elizabeth David. Her name crops up whenever the subject of twentieth-century food is mentioned, and when she died in 1992 an obituarist observed that she had done more to change British middle-class life than any poet, dramatist or novelist of the age. I'm keen to understand why she's held in such high regard and so she features on my list – *Cook three recipes from each chapter of an Elizabeth David book.*

By the time I get round to starting this project I've given up eating meat and so I forgo the pleasures of her classic books *French Country Cooking* and *Italian Food* in case they instruct me to pluck a pigeon; jug a wild hare; or boil, breadcrumb and grill a pig's trotter. Instead, I pick *Elizabeth David on Vegetables* which is a compilation of her vegetable recipes with chapters on soup, pasta, main courses, and side dishes. Rather more puzzling is the inclusion of chapters on puddings and bread.

I start out enthusiastically, cooking one or two dishes a week. But it doesn't go the way I expect. I note that a cold dish of button mushrooms stewed with olive oil, lemon juice, bay leaves and crushed coriander seeds is 'not bad.' I damn carrots in Marsala with faint praise. 'Pleasant flavour.' And green vegetable risotto gets a definite thumbs down. 'Dull and tasteless.' I follow her recipe for orange ice-cream using the traditional egg-yolk custard method and conclude that it has plenty of citrus flavour but is hard and icy. It's not a patch on Nigella's luscious, easy version made from oranges, icing sugar and double cream.

I'd expected to be roundly wowed but instead I'm underwhelmed and a bit annoyed. It feels sacrilegious to remain unmoved by a towering reputation but I can't help wondering how she became the *grande dame* of twentieth-century British cookery writing. And the answer is, of course, the same as with any kind of creative endeavour. It's largely about context. When was she writing? And who was she writing for?

Artemis Cooper's biography provides some of the answers and the first information of note is that she was born in 1913 to wealthy parents. Home was a Sussex manor house complete with a cook, nanny, governess, gardener and stable boy. In adulthood, she reminisced about how she took a great interest in the household's food but thoroughly disliked the dishes that Cook prepared for the nursery. 'Fish pudding with spiteful bones, boiled yellow marrows, overcooked parsnips, turnip tops, and repulsive puddings.' These included slimy junket, greasy jam roly-poly, and 'most revolting of all' – tapioca – which was apparently 'invented to torment children.'

Elizabeth was presented at Court and then went off to Paris to study art before trying her hand at acting and running off to Italy in a boat with her married lover. After their affair ended, she spent the Second World War in Greece and Egypt where she grew accustomed to sunshine, and fresh food full of flavour and colour. The range of ingredients was often limited but she observed how they were used in dish after dish with such skill that each appeared different. Meanwhile, wartime recipe books in Britain included instructions for crow boiled in suet, sparrow pie, and mock marzipan concocted from mashed haricot beans and a splash of almond essence.

After a brief marriage the young Mrs David returned to Britain and spent the winter of 1946-7 huddled up in a hotel in Ross-on-Wye. Not only was it the coldest time in living memory but post-war Britain was still under the grey thumb of rationing and she found the food stodgy, overcooked, and unimaginative. She started to write as a furious revolt against the cheerless, heartless food and the lack of sunshine. Even using the words apricot, olives, butter, rice, lemons, olive oil and almonds made her feel a bit better. She wrote vividly of where and when she had tasted and cooked various dishes, conjuring up images of blue seas, warm skies, and honest peasant traditions.

This writing formed the basis of her first volume, *A Book of Mediterranean Food* which was published in 1950, and was followed within a few years by *French Country Cooking* and *Italian Food*. There is no doubt that she was lucky in her timing. Her middle-class readers were hungry for fun and glamour, and travel was becoming more commonplace. She encouraged them to use good ingredients and to take trouble over cooking, presenting it as an act of creativity rather than a chore. It's hard to imagine a week when I don't use olive oil, aubergine, avocado, courgette, garlic, yoghurt, or basil but when Elizabeth David first started writing, these ingredients were largely unavailable and it was partly thanks to her influence that they started to appear in British shops.

It's helpful to learn more about the context in which she worked. We're on first name terms now and by the time I get to mushroom risotto, I'm warming to her. This is an outstanding recipe. In the past I've struggled to get flavour into a risotto but this manages it with a simple list of ingredients – olive oil, stock, mushrooms, onion, Italian rice, and garlic. Creamy, comforting and easy, I make it several times over the next few weeks and it always works out perfectly. That's a lesson I'm learning from her – restraint. She commented that as a nation we have a curious mistrust of the primitive and simple in food, and can't resist adding all sorts of ingredients and garnishes until in no time at all there are curry versions; cheese versions; super gigantic versions with bacon, lettuce, onion rings, and radishes – and their origins are no longer recognisable.

Other recipes that work well are a fresh tomato sauce, a gratin made from grated courgettes, and a Normandy apple tart sprinkled towards the end of its oven-time with buttery apple juices and a little sugar for crunch. There's restraint too in her sweet pepper and watercress salad. Just a shallot, half a bunch of watercress and fleshy red pepper, lightly dressed with lemon juice, olive oil, salt, and a pinch of sugar. The revelation is that the shallot is sliced paper-thin and the red pepper is cut into matchstick strips. The end result is beautifully balanced and so much more elegant than my usual sling-it-all-in affair. She doesn't give precise proportions for the dressing. This often happens in her writing. 'Leave a bit of space for people to make their own discoveries and use their intelligence. It makes it more fun,' she advised.

Despite this apparent license, she had many prickly opinions – garlic presses were 'utterly useless' and she refused to stock them in her kitchen equipment shop near to Sloane Square. Crinkly-rimmed china dishes were 'hideous.' What is more, 'Quiche Lorraine does NOT have cheese in it and should always be cooked in a tart tin.' She also said that the only acceptable use for rhubarb is in a fool. If only I could have a conversation with her, I'd say, 'But Elizabeth, you haven't tried my rhubarb crumble. Give the topping a bit of texture with Demerara sugar and *always* use wholemeal flour or it's too pallid. And you could add some sliced banana to the rhubarb and even a little finely diced stem ginger. It's delicious.' Sadly, I can imagine her tossing her head and snorting. Though hopefully she might give it a better review than when she reported that a Kensington restaurant served up some escalopes that could be veal, but could just as easily be the bedroom slippers that she threw away last week.

 I took her recipes at face value initially and was disappointed. And that's because she may be considered the best food writer of her generation but she is not of *my* generation. I can't re-create the heady excitement that her original readers must have felt, any more than I can empathise with the wicked thrill of early rock 'n' roll, or the incomprehension and outcry that greeted the first Impressionists. Elizabeth herself said there was little point in trying to reproduce dishes from one or two hundred years ago because our tastes change. And they change surprisingly quickly. I notice that some of the pages in my recipe file are now outdated. I doubt if I will eat meat again, so old favourites like pot roast, and cider sausage casserole are redundant. Some of the pudding recipes seem too sweet these days, and there was a time when I used to make spiced apricot chutney for the children to take as Christmas presents to teachers. There's a time and a place for everything and that's all in the past along with my ex-husband's favourite biscuits.

What is important is that Delia and Nigella built on the foundations she laid. And there's a similar story with Jane Austen and how her innovations paved the way for the modern novels I enjoy. Maybe there are some parallels too in family life. In the best of worlds each generation stands on the shoulders of the one that came before, introduces new ideas, and reaches higher.

Esmeralda's secrets

One of the disadvantages of being a late addition to my family is that I never met any of my grandparents. None of them survived into old age and so they were all gone by the time I was born. They weren't talked about much and as my parents had moved to a different part of the country, there was barely any connection to this earlier generation – just a few black and white photos. These were kept in a bureau drawer, jumbled in with all kinds of other things, and I'd occasionally open it and see my mother's parents. Her publican father, Ernest, beamed, almost bursting out of his waistcoat with bonhomie, while her mother Hilda stared at the camera, neither friendly nor severe, giving nothing away. I couldn't detect a physical resemblance to me, or anyone else in my family, and as their world of London pubs, the Blitz, and masonic dinners, seemed a long way from mine, I looked on them as a curiosity from another age.

It took a while to realise how disconnected I was from my family history. If you grow up knowing your grandparents, there's a reasonable chance they might tell you stories about their parents, and even grandparents, scooping you up in a continuity going back several generations, and providing a sense of where you come from. There was none of that in my family. I didn't even know where any of my grandparents were born and I took it for granted that this was how things were – as if it was an inevitable consequence of living in small-town Devon while the rest of my extended family lived in a place, vaguely referred to by my mother as 'the London area.'

It was having my own children that made me curious about my history. Parenting was raising questions in my mind about my attitudes to all kinds of things like fears, aspirations and health, and I wanted to understand more about where I'd come from and what I had unconsciously brought with me into this big, new adventure – one that carried so much responsibility for the next generation's happiness and well-being. But by the time I started wondering, my parents were dead and like so many of us, I regretted not asking questions while I had the chance. My father never said *anything at all* about his family – which now strikes me as strange – but my mother told occasional stories and so when I decided to embark on family history research, it was my maternal grandmother, the inscrutable Hilda, who first came under the spotlight. I was by then a strung-out mother of four and as I was always in a rush, I was amused to recall one of the few childhood stories that my mother told. Hilda would make elaborate party dresses but she always ran out of time, and so my mother and her sister would have to be pinned into their new clothes at the last minute. Many a party was spoiled by silent torture from invisible pins. While slapdashery may be a tenuous bond with my grandmother, it's better than nothing.

I started my family history research by taking out a subscription to Ancestry and searching online for birth, marriage, and death certificates, as well as census entries. And as I did so, I became increasingly perplexed by Hilda. Not only was she inscrutable but she was also proving to be extremely elusive. I went down a number of blind alleys before eventually uncovering a trail of secrets and false information. If official documents are to be believed, then almost nothing about my grandmother remained constant throughout her life. I think my mother would have been surprised to discover that Hilda was really named Esmeralda and that she was quite a few years older than she claimed to be. On the other hand, maybe those things are not that unusual – people are often coy about their age and it's not uncommon to go by another name. But I do think my mother would have been amazed to find out that Hilda was already married and living in Brighton when she met my grandfather. And I think she would have been absolutely astounded to discover that Hilda had four children from this first marriage. When she fled to London in 1919, about to be divorced by her husband, and leaving no forwarding address, she took her youngest child, Winifred, with her but left a boy and girl behind. There had been another little girl, Phyllis, but she had died several years before from gastroenteritis.

By the time she ran away with Ernest, Hilda was already pregnant with my mother, and they later had two more boys. So, although my mother went through her whole life thinking she was the second of four children she was, in fact, the fifth of seven. I think she would also have been stunned by the news that her parents did not get married until 1943, by which time she was twenty-four. This was done in secret – presumably everyone assumed they'd been married all along, and I surmise that with bombs falling all around them, it seemed wise to put their relationship on a secure footing. It feels odd that my mother went through seventy-eight years never knowing these facts, and yet by sitting at home tapping on my computer I have become privy to this personal information.

Exploring Esmeralda's life raised all kinds of questions and provided useful insight into my family history but she is only one part of the story and I know little about my grandfather Ernest – other than that he was a printer and laterally a publican, and that he was kind to my mother. So, uncovering something of his past is another project. It is on my list.

Hill is a common surname and I hit several blank walls using online resources. But it *is* all there to be found, and with a bit of patience, I eventually have details of Ernest and the three generations that precede him. How strange that he probably never knew the names of all of his eight great-grandparents, but I *do*. Not only are there Hills in my ancestry but there are also other common names – Weller, Perkins, Jarvis, Garland, Pierce and Atkinson. We're solidly working class with the men in occupations that include gardener, agricultural labourer, butcher, sailor, railway carriage cleaner, and wool stapler. Amongst the women's jobs are laundress, needlewoman and glove-maker. One branch comes from a constellation of Somerset villages, and another from the Witney area of Oxfordshire. Ernest, his parents, and his two grandmothers were all born in London. I'd like to feel some kind of connection with these names and occupations but they seem remote. And I have to wonder too, whether there is indeed a real connection. After all, it is estimated that somewhere between 3% and 13% of fathers cited on birth certificates are not the genetic father. We can trace our family tree but it only takes one instance of paternal discrepancy for those generations below to be completely unrelated to us. But at least with Ernest, given the circumstances of Esmeralda's divorce and the timing of my mother's birth, I can be pretty confident that *he* is related to me.

I get Ernest's family tree drawn up, printed and framed by a specialist service. Then I hang it on the wall in the downstairs loo. Seeing it there makes me feel more whole. I thought I'd explained what it was to my children, but I've clearly not made much fuss about it as recently Henry emerged from the loo, and asked, sounding mystified, 'Who is Ernest Hill?'

'He's your great-grandfather,' I was able to say with pride. 'And you have a great-grandmother called Esmeralda.' One day they might all value that continuity…

Experimenting with forgiveness

... because whether they like it or not there *is* a continuity. In the words of Saint Augustine – 'The dead are invisible; they are not absent.'

I doubt if my ancestors thought about unresolved trauma passing down the generations, but books like Bessel van der Kolk's *The Body Keeps the Score* and Mark Wolynn's *It Didn't Start With You*, argue that it's not easy or even possible, to differentiate what is ours, and what is not. Previous generations live with us like ghosts – crowding around, silently nudging us and turning our attention to *their* traumas and individual unhappinesses. They feed our deepest fears.

Take Esmeralda. Where does she fit in? When I started rummaging through her secrets, I thought of her as a mysterious character to whom I could play detective. A comical figure – my *naughty* grandmother. But although I've solved some puzzles and pinned down key dates, I don't have any personal documents like letters and diaries that might put flesh on her story. I just have a bunch of questions. Why did she abandon her two eldest children? Was she selfish? Was she scared? Was she emotionally frozen after the death of baby Phyllis? Was she helplessly, crazily in love with Ernest? And it's a short step from there to the pivotal questions that link her to my life and that of my children. What kind of mother was *she* to the mother who mothered *me*? My mother didn't say much but she did tell me that Esmeralda openly favoured her sons over her daughters. 'Oh, I love my *boys*,' she would say about her two youngest children. It still hurt my mother all those years later – was this where her self-confidence problems began?

And then there's the previous tier. What shaped *Esmeralda*? I doubt that she got off to a good start as she was the youngest of ten and her father died six weeks before she was born. Her mother worked as a seamstress but was an invalid by the 1891 census, when Esmeralda was three. What kind of mothering did Esmeralda get from an impoverished widow in poor health?

I can look back, but I also want to face forward as I know that my children are free to ask themselves what kind of mothering they've had from *me*. And what they have inherited. That makes me feel exposed and raw. Because when I ask *myself* that same question in relation to my own mother then I am overwhelmed by the things that I wish I *hadn't* inherited from her. Fear of bad luck. Fear of disappointment. Fear of nervous meltdown. Health anxieties. Self-doubt.

It's frustrating to realise that I've lived with these fears for all these years and have unconsciously allowed them to constrain and shape me. Especially since I've not been trapped like my mother was. I've had a good education, have the means to explore psychological well-being, and have benefited from improved rights for women. There have been highs and lows but for the most part my life has been way more emotionally and financially stable than that of my mother. And yet familial insecurities carve such deep furrows that for decades I have put my trust in crossing my fingers, tossing salt over my shoulder and keeping the magpies sweet. It took a straight-talking South African to call me out on *that*.

There are physiological factors at play, too, that are impossible to avoid. The developing foetus is affected by its mother's emotions because hormones cross the placenta. When my mother was expecting me, she was worried, unhappy and lonely so I can be sure there were plenty of fear and anger hormones swilling around. She too, in her own prenatal development will have been exposed to Esmeralda's stress as she fled her first marriage, left her children, and set up a new life with Ernest. And from the emerging field of epigenetics there are indications that anxiety can result in modifications to the genetic code and that these can pass down the generations.

Thinking like this puts a new perspective on my feelings about my parents. As humans we are all just links in our own family chains and our encumbrances are inherited involuntarily. Who can know exactly what my parents inherited, as well as having to cope in their own lives with poverty, lack of education, domestic violence and loneliness. They didn't have friends or family that they could share their burdens with and that makes me sad for them.

It's easy to focus on the flaws and mistakes as like so many parents of their generation, they behaved as though children were small creatures who were perplexing and inconvenient. But I don't want to fall into the trap of binary thinking and for the sake of my own wholeness, and to be fair to my mother's memory, I want to remember that she had many *good* characteristics. She was hard-working, funny, friendly, and polite. She could also be brave, accepting and grateful, and although she had little money, she managed it carefully so there was always food on the table and she was never in debt. Fundamentally, I do know that she loved me. We had the chance for some healing when Will was born as she came to stay for three months and looked after me – cooking delicious, nutritious food and making sure I got some rest. And over the following years as Nanny, she wrote letters to Will – playful, silly stories about his teddy bear and all the things she herself was doing. They were full of love and showed a side of her that she had not been able to indulge when I was a child.

I guess that what I'm exploring here is akin to forgiveness. I've struggled to know what that means and have imagined it as having an on-off switch so that I would know when I'd found it. But instead, I can see that it's a process of gradual change and acceptance. More than anything it's about understanding. Once I take the pressure of the f-word out of the equation then it suddenly becomes easier. It allows for nuance.

Something has also shifted in my attitude towards Shaun. He wanted something different and was not afraid of change in order to get it. Whereas I did not want change and *was* afraid of it. He could certainly have been kinder but marriages do crumble under pressure. And we bring our own vulnerabilities. It's just the way it is. Wounds can heal. I find myself wishing that things hadn't been so hard for him and not just because of the impact everything had on *me*.

I have to wonder what I will contribute to the next generations – what I have *already* contributed. My responsibility is not just to myself. Perhaps my worst fear about all of this is that my children will feel angry and disappointed in me as I did with *my* mother. I've been overwhelmed and made mistakes but I hope they understand that people are fallible, and that apologies help, and they are always loved. I would have liked to halt the intergenerational problems but it was too late to spot them all. All I can say is that I made some progress, and I see my children making yet more progress. Perhaps that is the point of life.

It's a glorious Spring afternoon. I'm having a day out in London and spend some time at Southwark Cathedral. The sun streams through the stained-glass windows. I see saints… angels…a lion…the Madonna and child. They're beautiful. I've never done this before but I put 50p in the collecting box and light a votive candle.

It's for my mum.

2019

Not the end

It's just a few weeks until my birthday – the big one – and there's just one treat left languishing on my list. A trip to Japan, because of all distant countries this is the one that intrigues me most. The culture feels familiar through all manner of curious words – *origami, kimono, geisha, sumo, sushi, bonsai, haiku* – and yet remains a conundrum because it's so different from the West.

It *would* be ideal to complete the list by my birthday, as I'd aspired to do when I made it all those years ago, but we've enjoyed so many treats over the past couple of years that I want to space them out a bit. Otherwise, they might stop feeling special. It doesn't come easily but after some tentative negotiation with myself bearing in mind those troublesome mindsets – completionism and rushing – I conclude that to have *made the booking* by my birthday will be good enough.

So now it's in the diary. We're going in April, and fortuitously that happens to be cherry blossom time. This means that all is going swimmingly in the list department. Except that is, for the one cloud that continues to cast a shadow – my relationship with the South West Coast Path. We're still on a break.

After the Prawle Point Incident, I returned home both disappointed in myself and with my trust in the Path in tatters. But like all hastily-ended love affairs there were questions to address and it wasn't long before I found myself wondering if other people struggle with this section.

I emailed the South West Coast Path Association and got a prompt reply from a manager named Mark. It was enormously helpful. 'That part near Gammon Head is probably the scariest bit of the entire path,' he wrote. 'I can't think of any other section where it's so narrow and so close to an edge.' He also named several other sections that I might find tricky – one on Exmoor, another at Lamorna in Cornwall, and a third near to St Aldhelm's Head in Dorset. I'd already done that last one, and since I had no memory of it, then I'd evidently coped. He ended by saying that in more than twenty years of managing the Prawle Point stretch of the path he was not aware of any accidents there. 'I think that because it's so challenging, people take extra care.'

I also did some research to try to understand what this fear of heights – acrophobia – is all about and discovered that its root is in perceptual differences. When there's a big empty space below with no landmarks to provide orientation, most people rely less on visual information and more on the information that comes from the balance-sensing organ of the inner ear together with feedback from the rest of their body about its position. But people with acrophobia continue to rely more heavily on visual information which leads to confusion and cognitive overload. One climbing website describes it as 'being captured by the empty space.'

'I've been thinking about your birthday,' says Mike. 'What would you like to do?'

'I want to have all the children to stay for a weekend,' I say somewhat predictably. 'And do you know... I think I'd like to spend my *actual* birthday on the Coast Path.'

He comes back later having done some research. 'How about Plymouth?' he says. 'I've never been but it looks interesting with plenty of history, *and* it's in your home county. The Coast Path goes right through it so we can try a bit and see how you feel.'

He organises everything and the day before my birthday we travel by train from Southampton to Plymouth. There's a dusting of snow in the fields as we pass through Wiltshire. He's booked a cosy city-centre flat and on the morning of my sixtieth birthday we have breakfast in a cafe overlooking Sutton Harbour and then take a breezy walk along the seafront. Plymouth Sound has seen some sights. Drake set off from here to do battle with the Spanish Armada, the Pilgrim Fathers set sail for the New World, and Napoleon Bonaparte was held here on a warship for ten days before his fate was decided and he was sent to St Helena. Thousands of people came, hoping to catch sight of their arch-enemy, Old Boney. Reports say that the weather was good, the ladies were brightly dressed, and a thousand boats bobbed around on the water with inevitable collisions and even several deaths.

Lunch is carrot cake and coffee from an organic pop-up stall at the Royal William Victualling Yard – a collection of grand limestone and granite buildings used for provisioning the Royal Navy for many years, and now redeveloped as restaurants, boutiques, and artists' studios. 'Happy birthday,' I hear someone say and look up but it's directed towards a young man at the next table. I'm very pleased as I've hardly ever met anyone who shares my birthday. I have an irrational belief that it is not a popular date though the actual day I was born *is* associated with a famous death. It even features in a well-known song – *American Pie*. I lean across and exchange birthday greetings with the young man. He looks about the same age as Buddy Holly was when he died so unexpectedly in a plane crash sixty years ago today.

The next day we decide to do some walking, and get a bus towards the twin villages of Kingsands and Cawsands, the former in Devon and the latter in Cornwall. It crosses the Tamar on the Torpoint Ferry and on the other side the lanes are narrow and cloaked with February fog as we bump along on the top deck catching occasional glimpses of the sea. Kingsands is charming with colourful cottages crowded around the small harbour and a house named Devon Corn because it stands on the county boundary. Today we have edged into Cornwall for the first time on our Coast Path walk. Our route takes us past Rame Head and back into Devon, and as we look out over the English Channel, my head is full of shipwrecks, smugglers, and Old Boney. We walk through woods and eventually reach Mount Edgcumbe Country Park with its Grade 1 listed gardens. These are home to the National Camellia Collection. I never expect to see much colour in Winter but we've come at exactly the right time to catch the camellias in exuberant displays of pink, scarlet, yellow, apricot, and white.

It's been a splendid day with no scary bits and I'm ready to commit to the Path again. But before we can carry on through Cornwall there's still some Devon coastline to fill in. So, in March we come back and pick up where we left off the previous autumn. I'm on my guard but all goes well until the middle of the afternoon when we come round a headland and I can see that the path on the opposite side of a small inlet looks high, exposed and narrow.

'I can't do it,' I state firmly. 'I'll walk up to the main road and go round.'

'If you really want to,' says Mike. 'But I think you'll regret it and it'll only make it worse next time you come across another bit like that.' I struggle between reason and panic and eventually decide that he's being very irritating but is probably right.

'OK' I say crossly. 'I'll do it. But I *really* don't want to and I'm going to keep my eyes on my feet so I don't have to look over the cliff.'

It takes all my concentration, and time does that annoying slowing-down thing so it seems to last for ages when it's probably less than five minutes. But amazingly, it works and I get to the end of the high track without having to cling to any rocks or cry. I'm euphoric to have a new strategy.

The Path may have thrown a few challenges into its heady mix but these *have* made it a deeper experience. I learned early on in my love affair with it that sometimes you're really tired and your feet are hurting but if you just keep putting one foot in front of the other, then eventually you get to the end of the day. I learned to pace myself too, especially with that *thirty steps, rest for five breaths* trick that got me up Golden Cap and other ascents.

It has also prompted me to recognise the difference between fear and anxiety. The first is a response to a current threat but anxiety is worrying about some threat that *might* happen in the future. Even though I was distressed at Prawle Point, the fear was useful, at least to some extent, as it made sure I tackled that section at a pace and level of caution that was within my capability. But when I got home the worry that it might happen again—the anxiety—nearly convinced me to give up. It was so thorough in its attempts to keep me safe that it erected a barrier between me and something I love.

It's important too to remember that I do have options. I *can* miss out sections if I feel I really need to. No-one will care. Except me. And so, I have to get into the mindset where I *won't* care. To be happy about what I do, not unhappy about what I don't. There are more important things to worry about than whether I do or don't cover every metre of the Coast Path. Climate change, far-right politics, family relationships, staying healthy… I need to keep a sense of perspective. And that leaves me with a convenient set of take-away messages. Convenient because they all happen to start with the letter P. Persistence. Patience. Pacing and Perspective. Thank you, South West Coast Path.

I'm so glad I didn't give up, and not least because this latest section brings the most wonderful moment so far. It happens at the point where the River Erme finishes its journey from Dartmoor and flows into the English Channel. When we arrive, the tide is out and the sand of the riverbed is completely exposed. It's safe to cross on foot, one hour either side of low tide, and this saves us a nine-mile detour around the estuary, so we remove our boots, tie the laces together and sling them round our necks. Then we take off our socks and roll our trousers up to our knees. The water is no more than ankle deep and we wade across the wide expanse between Wonwell and Mothecombe feeling fine streams of sand slide past our toes. It takes about five minutes and on the other side we dry our feet and take out our mid-morning coffee and shortbread. It's a picture-book Sunday morning with children squatting by rock pools and dogs dashing about. Then something happens that is so magical I can hardly believe what I'm seeing. Some horses appear, cantering along the riverbed, their heads held high and the wind in their manes. They're loving it and so are their riders. It's the embodiment of freedom and joy. And as suddenly as they appeared, they are gone.

Having never been able to pin my name to any sport or activity, I've now found one that haunts my daydreams and pulls me back for more. This walk is one of the best things I've ever done. And it's so much more than a walk – it's an absorbing book with the sea as the main protagonist and each mile of the plot introducing new themes and characters. Every time I stop, I put my metaphorical bookmark on the page and look forward to when I can pick it up again. I haven't finished but it doesn't matter. It just means there's more to enjoy before that sense of loss that comes with the end of the very best books.

The entire coastline of Cornwall beckons.

State of wonder

Travelling around Japan reminds me how it feels to be a small child. To be constantly coming across things that you've never encountered before. What's this? Why's it done like that? What are the rules? This is the most exciting thing about the trip – trying to see all manner of things from a different perspective and keeping an open mind. At home I spend a lot of time attempting to make sense of what's around me, but this is on a different scale.

We start with a couple of days in Tokyo and when we take a water bus across Tokyo Bay, I'm surprised to look back over a landscape dominated by soaring silver towers with little that looks traditional. This is partly down to the city's rapid expansion after the Second World War when Japan strove to demonstrate its modernity. But it's also because many thousands of old buildings were destroyed in two devastating events – in March 1945 when the US Army Air Forces carried out intense firebombing raids, and before that in 1923 when it was struck by the Great Kanto Earthquake.

History and geography inform here and they're at the root of many of the things that I'm puzzling over. It's true that they shape all countries but Japan has some specific challenges that I've not come across before. In a country where there's an ever-present threat to one's existence from earthquakes, tsunamis, typhoons, volcanic eruptions, floods and mudslides, then fleeting beauty is particularly poignant. It's why natural phenomena like a full moon, waves crashing on the shore, and cherry blossom are so revered. We're here during *hanami* – the festival of cherry blossom viewing – and it's clearly a big deal. The present moment is something to cherish.

We take a lunchtime walk through Ueno Park which has more than a thousand cherry trees. They're all in their pink and white party dresses, and the grass is crowded with groups sitting on picnic sheets covered in bento boxes, snacks, drinks, paper plates, and chopsticks. There's much good cheer and many people are in traditional dress – flowery kimonos for the women and plain, restrained styles for the men. Late that evening, we cut through the park on the way to our hotel and the parties are still in full swing. It's dark and the cherry trees are wearing lantern necklaces of red and orange.

The next day we're up promptly to explore Tsukiji, the old fish market with its narrow, crowded alleys. This is Tokyo's *Food Town* and we see huge crouching orange crabs, spiny vegetables, and great briny bags filled with tiny shrimps and baby flatfish. We reward ourselves for the early start with a sushi breakfast and I discover that I don't like sea urchin – in fact it's the worst thing I've ever tasted – but everything else is delicious even when I'm not sure what it is. There's lots of fish and lots of rice. Before this holiday I'd just assumed that was what Japanese people like to eat but I'd not taken the geography into account. It makes perfect sense for an island nation to harvest what it can from the sea, and because much of the soil is thin and there's relatively little grassland on which to graze livestock, farmers choose crops that suit the terrain – rice paddies can be terraced into the slopes of mountains.

Indeed, about two-thirds of the land is rocky and mountainous and this has resulted in urban settlements being crowded into the valleys and along the coast. With high population density in these areas, then domestic space is at a premium and this affects lifestyle in countless ways. Restaurants, for example. Japan has the highest number per capita of any country in the world because people rarely entertain at home, and it's no coincidence that it produced Marie Kondo, the world's most famous decluttering enthusiast.

We leave Tokyo on a Shinkansen train. It's comfortable, and efficiency is highly valued with one train operator recently releasing a statement apologising for the 'great inconvenience we placed upon our customers... it was truly inexcusable.' All because the train had left twenty seconds early. We're on our way to the Japanese Alps where we are staying in a traditional mountain inn – *ryokan* – and the final part of our journey into the mountains is by bus. We check in at reception and then a grey-haired lady in a kimono appears and leads us to our room. She gestures for us to sit at the low black lacquered table while she prepares some green tea. Then she leaves and we sit, taking in the views of trees and mountains and enjoying the shadows cast by the paper-paned shutters. We each have a bean paste sweet – a yellow chick and a purple wisteria flower.

After a while, the kimono lady returns carrying a pile of lavender-coloured fabric. She places it on the table, looks Mike up and down, makes a worried face and then shuffles out of the room backwards while bowing. We wait, wondering what will happen next. A few minutes later she reappears and explains with gestures and a demure giggle that Mike is tall and so she had to go and fetch a bigger size. She selects mine from the pile – a *yukata* which is like a kimono but more suited to casual occasions. I put it on and she places a striped woven belt around my waist, drawing it together and indicating that I should tie it. I do my best but bow-tying is not one of my talents and she looks unhappy with my effort. She reties it with deft efficiency before standing back, giving me an exacting appraisal and nodding. Then she gives me a silky green jacket to slip on top, and a pair of opaque white socks. Meanwhile Mike has been busy putting on his *yukata* and taking care to wrap it left over right – not the other way as that's used for dressing the dead.

Now that we're properly dressed, we set off to explore the *onsen* – baths fed by hot volcanic springs and one of the few reasons to celebrate Japan's geological hazards. But we don't stay dressed for long as you have to bathe naked. There are separate baths for men and women but also a couple of private baths for couples and families. In Japan, people might baulk at a husband and wife greeting one another in public with a kiss but nudity is associated with health and cleanliness – it's more acceptable to expose your body than to expose what's going on in your heart or mind. It's essential to be clean before you enter the water and so we have to prepare in the indoor washing area. Mike sits on one of the wooden stools and immediately falls off. What looked like the seat was in fact an upturned bowl for rinsing yourself. We finally get into the bath which is surprisingly hot and is landscaped with rocks, bamboo, azaleas and ferns. It's sublime.

In the evening, we go down to the dining room where our table is laid out with about twenty small bowls and dishes containing sushi, sashimi, a savoury custard, delicate carved vegetables, bean curd, sticky rice, pickles, and miso. There are tiny claw forks for excavating crab meat, and a pot of broth simmering on a burner. There's so much to try but one thing we must not do is to pass food to one another using our chopsticks. That's only done at funerals. We drink sake and plum wine and finish with fluorescent green melon.

Our next journey involves three buses and a train. We're on our way to Matsumoto to see the black Crow Castle and just when I'm starting to feel sick because the mountain road is so twisty, we come round yet another bend and I forget my nausea because there ahead of us is Mount Fuji. It's unmistakeable and ravishing with snow drizzling down the slopes like a fancy pudding, and a fluffy garnish of cloud on top. In the busy town of Gotemba we change buses and when we glance along a street cluttered with a tangle of overhead cables and a pylon, there filling the view like decoupage pasted onto the sky is this magnificent conical icon. I'm astonished to feel so moved by it.

There's an embarrassing moment when we check into our accommodation in the city of Kanazawa. It all starts well when our host, Suko, opens the door of his compact house and greets us with a low bow from the waist. He is solemn and although he doesn't smile, I understand enough to know that he is giving us a fulsome welcome. I want to return the friendly sentiment but get confused and my hand shoots out. I immediately wonder why I did that when I rarely go for the formality of a handshake at home, and here I am in a country where physical contact is largely avoided. Suko looks horrified but is above all polite, and so he puts his hand out tentatively and we perform a loose, awkward handshake, getting it over with as quickly as possible.

Then he takes a cloth and wipes the wheels of our suitcases. He gestures to a shelf where we are to put our shoes and he hands us some slippers. Not for the first time this week I'm pleased to be wearing pumps as we're taking our shoes on and off such a lot. Homes are special areas, separate from the dirt, chaos and danger of the outside world and one of the ways to mark this is to leave your shoes at the door. In some places you even have to rinse your mouth before entering.

The *onsen* has given us a taste for Japanese bathing so when we get to Kyoto we seek out the nearest *sento* public bathhouse. We arrive at about ten in the evening and it's busy. With pressure on domestic space some homes still do not have bathrooms but *sento* are also important for social and community reasons. I'm the only Westerner in the female baths but it feels companionable with women scrubbing one another's backs and gossiping. A mother is dressing two little girls in pink pyjamas and I sit next to a woman who is cleaning herself meticulously. I wash with what I consider to be adequate care, bathe for some time in several different baths and then wash my hair. When I get back, she's still washing.

Our last destination is Hiroshima and as the train approaches, I feel uncomfortable that it has become a tourist destination, and that we're part of that. But like most visitors I'm here because I want to understand more about its place in twentieth-century history. Our walk from the station to our accommodation takes us through the longest shopping mall I've ever seen and this comes as a surprise. It's as if I'm expecting to find everything in suspended animation whereas in reality this is a modern city that has had to grow out of its painful ashes and is home to more than a million people.

There are reminders everywhere though, and the first we come across is the A-Bomb Dome which was once an exhibition hall with a distinctive green dome. It was engulfed by flames when the bomb dropped and everyone inside died instantly, but despite the devastation its position immediately below the blast resulted in some of the walls remaining upright, and the skeleton iron frame of the dome is still in place. Many people called for it to be demolished but it stays here, looking exactly as it did immediately after the bombing with its hollow centre, charred stonework and random chunks of rubble around the base.

At the Peace Memorial Park, we see a young man in shorts and sneakers chanting over the Memorial Mound which contains the ashes of 70,000 unidentified victims. And nearby in the Peace Memorial Museum we read accounts from bomb survivors. They are hellish. The following morning, we join a handful of other tourists waiting by the river to hear the Peace Clock Tower chime its prayer of peace. It does this every morning at 8.15 to mark the time when the bomb was dropped. We all sit, still and silent as the bells sing out sweetly like a carillon, and people hurry past on their way to work.

Afterwards we get the train to Tokyo for our flight home. It's been a sobering morning but this seems fitting for the final chapter of the final treat on my list. I've always felt uncomfortable about the connotations of luxury and indulgence that the word *treat* conjures up but have never been able to come up with anything better. These treats provided a lifeline when I was desperate and as things gradually improved, they continued to work their magic. I'm so grateful for that.

And now what…?

Epilogue: A new list

Well, this is what…
    On my sixtieth birthday I give myself a present of a new list – 70 before 70. I want to walk around the coast of the Isle of Wight, do a silent retreat, kayak on the Wye, go to the Sistine Chapel, revisit my favourite childhood books, take the Oslo to Bergen train, the Bernina Express, go to a Quaker meeting, learn the Charleston, get to know a couple of Sondheim musicals, watch (all of) Marilyn Monroe's films, learn some magic tricks, go to Vietnam, Georgia, the Amalfi Coast… and so much more.

My last list was there beside me during a period of great change. It was a reassuring structure. It signposted new experiences and ideas. And it was buried treasure. I hope that this new one will similarly entreat me to live life vividly.

In the classic *New Passages*, Gail Sheehy writes that when we pass from one stage of life to another, we shed our protective hard shell as a lobster does, and we are left exposed and vulnerable until a new covering grows. At these points we are also yeasty and embryonic and enjoy a heightened potential for growth. I'm not sure I like the image of being yeasty but in other ways it describes pretty well what these past few years have been about.

Towards the end of writing this book I came across *When I Grow Up: Conversations With Adults in Search of Adulthood* by psychotherapist, Moya Sarner. She asks what it means to be a grown-up – something I've wondered all my life. Clearly, it's not about whether you have contents insurance, host dinner parties, pay into a pension, or do DIY. When I got married at the age of twenty-four and then when I had my first baby aged twenty-nine, I thought these things would make me into a grown-up. But they didn't. So, what is it and how do you know if you're properly grown up? The answer I am most convinced by is that you don't ever reach a fixed, definable state of grown-upness because you and the demands on you, keep changing. Instead, we have to *keep* growing up. Or attempting to. Over and over again. Facing up to challenges, meeting them squarely and making psychological leaps. Otherwise, we remain stuck. Her name for this kind of leap is a grow-up.

Sarner describes many characteristics of being a grown-up – developing a capacity to bear emotional pain rather than running away from it, seeing oneself as separate from loved ones, tolerating imperfection and uncertainty, accepting difference in others, accepting the need for help from others, developing the awareness to become the person you are rather than the one others want you to be, accepting some things are out of your control and that losses have to be mourned, and taking responsibility for yourself rather than blaming your limitations on others while also knowing that sometimes we are subject to the decisions of others and are not responsible for those decisions.

I recognise many of these. Because that's what this story has been about. It has been a collection of grow-ups and out of my treats list has grown a new and very different kind of list – in fact not so much a list but more a toolkit for how to untangle some of the fears and thinking patterns that have bent me out of shape and blocked my path to grow-ups:-

> *Resist the story*
>
> *Challenge completionism*
>
> *Let go of resentment*
>
> *Tell my jostling thoughts to form an orderly queue*
>
> *Be alert to people-pleasing tendencies*
>
> *Name other emotional traps so I can spot them*
>
> *Seek simplicity*
>
> *Remember that life is a cycle of things coming together and falling apart again*
>
> *Be happy about the things I do, not regretful about those I don't*
>
> *Give complicated emotions time to unfold*
>
> *Exercise a growth mindset not a fixed one*
>
> *Call out foreboding joy and stop it in its tracks*

There's a significant moment one morning when I'm out for a walk on the Common and spot a small grey and black dog. Even though it may actually have the sweetest nature, it's got a beard and bristly eyebrows that make it look decidedly grumpy. I think it's a schnauzer. The owner is wandering along slowly, a short distance ahead but it's clearly agitated about something as it's yapping and making jerky, hesitant movements. As I get near, I see that the dog is goading a large magpie who looks ruffled but is holding its ground and strutting up and down assertively on the grass in front of some bushes. It has a smart black bib, a pristine white undercarriage, and glossy petrol-blue wings. Maybe it's protecting a nest behind the bushes. I watch with admiration, realising that the dog looks more nervous than the bird and as my hand starts to lift automatically to my head in salute, I stop and place it firmly back in my coat pocket. I don't need to do that anymore.

In the year following my birthday I pluck some treats from the new list. I spend a Spring afternoon at the National Theatre watching Stephen Sondheim's *Follies*. I go on my own and thoroughly enjoy it. A few weeks later Mike and I do some kayaking on the Wye. I thoroughly enjoy that too. Then we go to Rome and the Sistine Chapel. It's glorious – of course. I watch some of Marilyn Monroe's lesser-known films. Very interesting and I look forward to seeing more. One Sunday morning I sit in the safe, heavy silence of a Quaker meeting. I might go back.

I'm glad to have done all of these things. But gradually I begin to acknowledge that something's missing. And I realise that I don't have a pressing need for structure anymore. It simply seems to have evaporated. Instead of brimming with enthusiasm and excitement about all the things I could do, I'm going through the motions of engaging with my list. I'm feeling it's something I *ought* to be doing. Because it's a *list*. And *I've* written it. Somehow this one has come into the world as a demanding To-Do List whereas its older sibling was an easy-going Treats List.

Molly asked me recently whether I'd enjoyed having small children. I replied that I'd enjoyed it very much but am glad that she and her siblings are now grown-up, and she looked a bit hurt. But when I asked if she would like to go back to primary school and do it all again, then she understood – even though she'd enjoyed it. There's a time and a place.

I've changed and the world has changed. I'm questioning now whether I want to indulge all those climate-damaging air miles to Vietnam, for example, when I'd be quite happy walking on the UK coast or exploring Europe by train. I've no doubt that I'll continue picking off some of the ideas on my 70 List but whereas the earlier one was pinned to the wall above my desk this one is hidden away inside my computer. And the truth is that I'm not sure I want to learn any magic tricks. Or the Charleston. I'm not even sure I want a list anymore.

I bet you weren't expecting that. Not from a dyed-in-the-wool list addict.

Well, all I can say is that *I* wasn't either.

Life is full of surprises.

Appendices

The Complete List of 60 Treats

29 in *How I Learned to Stop Saluting Magpies*

- North Downs Way
- The Jewel in the Crown
- Cryptic crosswords
- Poundbury
- Glastonbury Festival
- Billy Wilder
- Knit a jacket
- Berlin
- Life on Earth
- Denis Severs' House
- Cook ten different kinds of fish
- Hitchcock
- Jane Austen's novels
- Produce a piece of art
- The Netherlands on my own
- Burgh Island Hotel
- South West Coast Path
- Middlemarch
- Find a clock with a nice tick
- The Camargue

- Dublin
- Norfolk Broads
- New England in the Fall
- American sleeper train
- St Petersburg
- River cruise
- Elizabeth David recipes
- Family tree
- Japan

31 in *31 Treats And A Marriage*

- New York
- Tate Liverpool
- Brideshead Revisited
- London Jewish walk
- Old-fashioned roses
- Saki
- Theatre Royal Stratford
- Self-guided London walk
- Go to the races
- Go to a jazz club
- Sew a patchwork cushion
- Spa wrap treatment
- Greenwich market
- Make chocolate truffles
- Learn about birdsong
- Learn how to download digital photographs
- Make compost
- National Media Museum

- Learn about perfume
- Eye make-up
- Magic Circle evening
- Cirque du Soleil
- Derren Brown
- River Cafe Recipes
- Edinburgh
- Chatsworth
- Mad Men
- Zara
- Tallinn
- Riding lessons
- Port Sunlight

Fish recipes

All recipes serve two people and unless stated otherwise are my own.

Skate with black butter

"Why's it called black butter?" asked Molly. "It's brown". And so it is. Nut brown. If it goes black, then you've burnt it.

This is adapted from a recipe in *Delia Smith's Complete Cookery Course*. It's the book that taught me to cook thirty years ago. My copy is now in two halves and the backbone is missing. Many of the recipes have scribbled notes next to them and there are unidentifiable stains all over it. Emma has offered to buy me a pristine copy as a Christmas present, but I'm very attached to this old one and could never part with it.

- 2 skate wings
- 1 tablespoon sunflower oil
- 50g butter
- 1 tablespoon white wine vinegar
- 2 teaspoons capers
- Salt and pepper
- Flat leaf parsley, chopped for garnishing
- A lemon
- Heat the oven to 200°C/gas mark 6.

Season the skate wings. Heat the oil in a pan and fry the fish for a couple of minutes on each side until slightly browned. Transfer to a roasting pan and put in the oven for about 7-8 minutes. You'll know it's cooked when the flesh comes away from the bone easily.

Meanwhile, take a small saucepan and gently melt the butter in it. Then pour the yellow liquid into a second small saucepan making sure to leave the sediment behind. Heat the butter until it's nut brown but be careful not to let it go too far and burn. Add the vinegar and capers and season with salt and pepper.

Place the fish on warmed plates and pour the black butter over it. Sprinkle with the chopped parsley and place a lemon quarter on the side.

We had this with steamed spinach. Also mashed sweet potato with some freshly grated nutmeg and a light seasoning of salt and pepper.

Scallops with a tomato and herb dressing

This is adapted from a recipe in *Rick Stein's French Odyssey*.

- 8 large scallops with the pink coral still attached
- 2 tablespoons olive oil, plus one extra teaspoon for cooking the scallops
- 2 garlic cloves, crushed
- 3 medium vine tomatoes, skinned, deseeded and chopped finely
- ¼ teaspoon dried Herbes de Provence
- ¼ teaspoon caster sugar

- A small squeeze of lemon juice
- Snipped chives to serve

Gently heat 2 tablespoons of the oil, the garlic, tomatoes, Herbes de Provence, and sugar in a small saucepan for 5-10 minutes until the tomatoes are softened and the sauce is well combined. Add the lemon juice, then season to taste. Keep warm on one side while you cook the scallops.

Heat the remaining oil in a frying pan. Slice the scallops in two, horizontally, leaving the coral attached to one half. Season lightly with salt and pepper. Take eight halves and fry over a high heat for one minute. Flip them over and do the same on the other side. Remove from the pan and keep warm whilst you do the remaining eight halves.

Divide the scallops between two warmed plates. Drizzle the tomato sauce over them, and sprinkle with the chives.

Rick Stein suggests serving these with Puy lentils. I used a pack of Merchant Gourmet ready-prepared Puy lentils which can be heated through in a microwave in just a couple of minutes and are delicious. We had cauliflower on the side, cooked until soft and then whizzed in a food processor with a little olive oil and seasoning.

Baked monkfish

Monkfish is notoriously ugly but this doesn't matter as by the time you buy it at the fish counter the tail will have been cut into chunky fillets that look more inviting. It's easy to bake in the oven. And there are no bones. Hurray! This is based on a recipe in *The River Café Cookbook* by Rose Gray and Ruth Rogers.

- 2 pieces of monkfish fillet, each about 200g
- 2 teaspoons chopped fresh rosemary
- 65g butter
- A splash of white wine
- Half a lemon
- Salt and pepper

Heat the oven to 200°C/gas mark 6.

Take a small sharp knife and cut into the membrane around the fish. It's a bit like a very fine silk stocking. Take as much of it off as you can without damaging the fish too much.

Cut two rectangles of cooking foil which are big enough to make parcels for the fish. Put shiny side down on a baking tray and brush the inside with oil. Place a fish fillet in the centre of each and season well with salt and pepper. Add the chopped rosemary and divide the butter between them. Add a small squeeze of lemon to each. Fold the foil so that it makes a parcel but before closing completely add a splash of white wine to each. Bake in the oven for about 20 minutes. Open the parcels, place the fish onto warmed plates, and pour the juices over.

We had this with some courgettes, sliced and lightly fried in olive oil until just starting to brown. Also, a side salad of watercress and avocado dressed with a splash of olive oil, a small squeeze of lemon juice and some salt and pepper.

Fresh tuna on a bed of beans

Tuna is quick and easy to cook. It's also firm-fleshed and has no bones. Another hurray!

This recipe is adapted from 'thon aux deux haricots' in *The French Market* by Joanne Harris and Fran Warde. Reading this book makes me feel like I'm on holiday.

- 2 tuna steaks
- 80g French beans, trimmed and cut into half lengths
- 80g tinned haricot beans, drained
- 200g (half a tin) good quality chopped tomatoes, ideally cherry ones
- 2 cloves of garlic, crushed
- Salt and pepper
- 2 springs of basil for garnishing

Cook the French beans in boiling water for a few minutes until cooked, but so they still have a bit of bite in them. Drain and keep on one side. Heat the tomatoes and garlic together for about five minutes until slightly thickened. Season well with salt and pepper. Add the haricot beans and fold in the French beans. Keep warm. Meanwhile heat a little olive oil in a thick pan and when it's hot put the tuna steaks in. Watch carefully. I like mine well done so gave them 4 minutes each side. For medium give them 3 minutes, and if you're brave and like them rare, then they'll need just 2 minutes each side. Warm your plates and divide the bean mixture between them. Top with the tuna steaks and a sprig of basil.

We had this with some sweet potatoes, skins gently scrubbed and rubbed with a little olive oil, then roasted in the oven until soft.

Lemon sole fish fingers

For this dish you'll need to buy lemon sole fillets but it's worth being aware that it's very difficult to remove the skin before cooking. When I asked if the fish counter assistant could do this for me, she pursed her lips and shook her head. The dark upper side of the fish is there to provide camouflage but grey skin rather spoils the finished dish. It's better to ask for fillets from the underside as the skin is white and isn't so obvious.

- 2 lemon sole fillets, preferably from the white underside
- 1 tablespoon plain white flour
- 1 egg
- 50g fine breadcrumbs. I like Japanese panko crumbs.
- Sunflower oil for frying
- Salt and pepper
- 1 lemon

My fillets had a few fine bones in, so it's worth going over them carefully with your fingers and a pair of tweezers. Trim the thin edges using kitchen scissors, then cut the fillets into strips about 1cm wide. Get three small bowls. Put the flour in one, the beaten egg in the second, and the breadcrumbs in the third. Dip the fillets in the flour. Then season well with salt and pepper. Dunk in the egg and then roll gently in the breadcrumbs. Heat the oil in a frying pan and when it's hot, put the fish in. Fry gently and turn over until both sides are golden brown. Drain on kitchen paper and serve with a wedge of lemon on the side, some French fries or sweet potato chips, and peas or salad.

Spiced sea bream fillets on thyme and beetroot lentils

- 2 sea bream fillets
- 1 teaspoon tikka masala curry paste
- 1 teaspoon plain yogurt
- Half a lemon
- 2 medium cooked beetroot, chopped very finely
- 1 flavoursome medium tomato, chopped very finely
- 1 tablespoon fresh thyme, chopped finely
- 6 walnuts, chopped roughly
- Salt and pepper
- 400g tin green lentils, drained

Put the fish fillets skin-side down on a greased baking tray. Mix the curry paste and yogurt together and smear thinly over the fish. Squeeze just a little lemon juice over it. Put under a hot grill for about 6-8 minutes, watching carefully. It's ready when the skin flakes easily.

Meanwhile put the chopped beetroot and tomato into a small saucepan. Season well with salt and pepper and stir. Add the chopped thyme and the lentils. Heat through gently while the fish is cooking. Add the walnuts just before serving. Divide the lentil mixture between two warmed plates. Then place the fish on top.

We had this with yellow spiced basmati rice cooked with a stick of cinnamon, 6 cloves and ¼ teaspoon turmeric. And some steamed green beans.

Hake with peppers and very garlicky garlic bread

- 2 hake fillets with the skin on
- 2 teaspoons red pesto
- 1 red pepper
- 1 orange pepper
- 1 yellow pepper
- Olive oil
- 2 teaspoons paprika
- 1 small ciabatta loaf
- 75g butter, softened
- 4 cloves garlic crushed
- Salt and pepper
- Flat leaf parsley to garnish

Heat the oven to 200°C/gas mark 6.

Mix the butter and garlic together in a bowl. Slice the ciabatta into medium thick slices. Spread both sides of each slice generously with the garlic butter. Stick the slices back together into a loaf shape and wrap in foil to make a parcel. Place on a baking tray.

Season the hake with salt and pepper and place each fillet on a piece of cooking foil. Spread the pesto thinly over the fish. Fold the foil to make a parcel and place in a baking dish. Put both the bread and the fish in the oven and bake for about 15 minutes. The fish is ready when it breaks into flakes easily and the bread needs to be baked until the edges are beginning to get slightly crisp.

Meanwhile wash, halve and deseed the peppers. Then slice into strips. Heat the oil in a saucepan and add the pepper strips. Season, add the paprika and cook gently until soft. This will take about 15 minutes.

Serve the fish on a bed of peppers with a garnish of parsley and the garlic bread on the side.

Marinated swordfish steaks with garlic mushroom rice

- 2 swordfish steaks
- 1 lemon
- 3 tablespoons chilli-infused olive oil for the marinade
- 250g chestnut mushrooms, roughly chopped
- 2 cloves of garlic, crushed
- A little olive oil or sunflower oil for cooking the fish
- 8 fl oz basmati rice
- A bunch of chives, chopped, or a handful of wild garlic leaves roughly chopped
- 2 sprigs of mint
- Salt and pepper

Squeeze one tablespoon of lemon juice into a shallow bowl and add the chilli oil. Mix to combine. Then put the swordfish steaks into the bowl and leave to marinate – ideally for at least 30 minutes. Remove and season well. Heat the olive oil or sunflower oil in a frying pan and add the fish. I cooked mine for about 4 minutes each side, but you could give it less if you prefer it slightly pink in the middle.

Cook the rice in double its volume of water and add three-quarters of a teaspoon of salt. Meanwhile heat the olive oil or sunflower oil in a frying pan and sauté the mushrooms and garlic until cooked through. Add the chives or wild garlic leaves. If using wild garlic then heat the mixture for a couple of minutes until the leaves have wilted. Add the mushroom mixture to the cooked rice and fold through. Serve alongside the fish and garnish with a sprig of mint. We had this with sautéed courgettes.

Coconut Thai sea bass with rice noodles

- 2 sea bass fillets
- 400ml can coconut milk
- 3 tablespoons Thai green curry paste
- 3 teaspoons Thai fish sauce
- 1 medium carrot cut into thin sticks
- Half a head of broccoli broken into small florets
- 200g flat rice noodles
- 50g salted peanuts, chopped finely
- Basil to garnish

Steam the carrot and broccoli until cooked but still with a bit of bite to them. Put the coconut milk in a large pan and heat through. Stir in the curry paste and the fish sauce. Add the sea bass and cook gently for about 4 minutes or until it flakes easily. Meanwhile cook the rice noodles according to the instructions on the packet. Put the carrot and broccoli in the pan with the fish and serve onto a bed of noodles. Garnish with the basil and chopped peanuts.

Simply roasted turbot

- 1 medium turbot, filleted
- 2 garlic cloves cut into slivers
- 50g butter
- A splash of white wine
- Salt and pepper
- Sliced lemon and parsley to serve

Preheat the oven to 180°C/gas mark 4. Using sharp kitchen scissors trim away the fins and tail. Cut off the head if you or your eating companion are squeamish. Wash the fish and dry carefully with kitchen paper. With the white side up, make some slashes in the flesh and insert a sliver of garlic into each. Season well and put in a roasting dish. Dot the butter over it and add the wine. Put in the oven and leave to cook for about 30 minutes. Test the thickest area to see if it flakes easily, meaning it is cooked. If the edges are drying out then cover the fish loosely with cooking foil until it is ready. Serve on a warmed plate, garnished with the lemon slices and parsley. Each person can then help themselves by removing the fish from the bones.

We had this with mashed sweet potato and spinach.

Further Reading

I read dozens of books for inspiration and clarification, while I was writing this. Here in no particular order are those that I found especially useful.

Walking

North Downs Way: National Trail Guide—Colin Saunders

Wanderlust: A History of Walking—Rebecca Solnit

Walking the South West Coast Path—Paddy Dillon

Reverse Guide: South Haven Point to Minehead—The South West Coast Path Association

Solitude

Alone Time: Four seasons, Four Cities and the Pleasures of Solitude—Stephanie Rosenbloom

How to Be Alone—Sara Maitland and The School of Life

Quiet: The Power of Introverts in a World that Can't Stop Talking— Susan Cain

Intimacy & Solitude—Stephanie Dowrick

Friendship

Friends: Understanding the Power of our Most Important Relationships—Robin Dunbar

India

Paul Scott: A Life—Hilary Spurling

The Jewel in the Crown—Paul Scott

Glastonbury

Glastonbury: The Complete History of the Festival—John Bailey

Billy Wilder

Nobody's Perfect: Billy Wilder, A Personal Biography—Charlotte Chandler

Knitting

Zen and the Art of Knitting—Bernadette Murphy

Berlin

Oranges for Christmas: A Berlin Wall Escape Novel—Margarita Morris

Architecture

The Architecture of Happiness—Alain de Botton

Fish cookery

Rick Stein's French Odyssey—Rick Stein
The French Market—Fran Warde and Joanne Harris
Delia Smith's Complete Cookery Course—Delia Smith
The River Café Cookbook—Rose Gray and Ruth Rogers

Simplicity

Earthed: A Memoir—Rebecca Schiller

Dennis Severs' House

18 Folgate Street: The Life of a House in Spitalfields—Dennis Severs

Alfred Hitchcock

Alfred Hitchcock—Peter Ackroyd

Jane Austen

Jane Austen: A Life—Claire Tomalin

Elizabeth David

Writing at the Kitchen Table: The Authorised Biography of Elizabeth David—Artemis Cooper
Elizabeth David on Vegetables—Elizabeth David
Is There a Nutmeg in the House?—Elizabeth David

The Netherlands

Why the Dutch Are Different: A Journey into the Hidden Heart of The Netherlands—Ben Coates

Slow living

In Praise of Slow: How a Worldwide Movement Is Challenging the Cult of Speed—Carl Honoré

Middlemarch

The Road to Middlemarch: My Life with George Eliot—Rebecca Mead.

Norfolk Broads

Norfolk Broads—Collins Nicholson Waterways Guides

Coot Club—Arthur Ransome. Mentions the Swan Inn at Horning where we had the silent drama with the old gentleman.

Burgh Island Hotel

The Great White Palace—Tony Porter

Travel

The Art of Travel—Alain de Bouton

Ireland

A Pocket History of Ireland—Joseph McCullough

1916: A Novel of the Irish Rebellion—Morgan Llywelyn

St Petersburg

St Petersburg: Three Centuries of Murderous Desire—Jonathan Miles

Natasha's Dance: A Cultural History of Russia—Orlando Figes

Time

Time Warped: Unlocking the Mysteries of Time Perception—Claudia Hammond

Family

The Body Keeps the Score: Mind, Brain and Body in the Transformation of Trauma—Bessel van der Kolk

It Didn't Start with You: How Inherited Family Trauma Shapes Who We Are and How to End the Cycle—Mark Wolynn

Every Family Has a Story: How We Inherit Love and Loss—Julia Samuel

Parenthood

My Wild and Sleepless Nights: A Mother's Story—Clover Stroud

The Mother Dance: How Children Change Your Life—Harriet Lerner

Love

The Course of Love—Alain de Botton

Forgiveness, meaning and self-compassion

No Future Without Forgiveness—Desmond Tutu

Man's Search for Meaning—Viktor E. Frankl

Self Compassion: The Proven Power of Being Kind to Yourself—Kirsten Neff

The Compassionate Mind—Paul Gilbert

What's It All About?: Philosophy and the Meaning of Life—Julian Baggini

Perfectionism

The Perfectionist's Guide to Losing Control—Katherine Morgan Schafler

Japan

Dogs and Demons: The Fall of Modern Japan—Alex Kerr

The Rough Guide to Japan—Rough Guides

A Beginner's Guide to Japan: Observations and Provocations—Pico Iyer

Happiness and general ideas about how to live well

The Paradox of Choice: Why More is Less—Barry Schwarz

Happy Ever After: Escaping the Myth of the Perfect Life—Paul Dolan

Authentic: How to be yourself and why it matters—Stephen Joseph

The Wisdom of Insecurity: A Message for an Age of Anxiety—Alan Watts

Happy Money: The Science of Smarter Spending—Elizabeth Dunn and Michael Norton

Carpe Diem Regained: The Vanishing Art of Seizing the Day—Roman Krznaric

The Happiness Curve: Why Life Gets Better After Midlife—Jonathan Rauch

When Things Fall Apart: Heart Advice for Difficult Times—Pema Chodron

Back to Sanity: Healing the Madness of Our Minds—Steve Taylor

Life in Five Senses: How Exploring the Senses Got Me Out of My Head and Into the World—Gretchen Rubin

Finding Meaning in the Second Half of Life—James Hollis

Four Thousand Weeks: Embrace your limits. Change your life. Make your four thousand weeks count—Oliver Burkeman

Ways of thinking

Mindset—Carol Dweck

The Expectation Effect: How Your Mindset Can Transform Your Life—David Robson

Daring Greatly: How the Courage to Be Vulnerable Transforms the Way We Live, Love, Parent, and Lead—Brené Brown

Change

This Too Shall Pass: Stories of Change, Crises and Hopeful Beginnings—Julia Samuel

New Passages: Mapping Your Life Across Time—Gail Sheehy

When I Grow Up: Conversations with Adults in Search of Adulthood—Moya Sarner

Acknowledgements

Thank you to the many friends and family members who have enquired about the progress of this book over the four years it has taken to write. I really do appreciate the curiosity and engagement, and hope the final product is worth waiting for. I am especially indebted to those friends who accompanied me on individual treat adventures – Caroline Norman, Claire Jackson, Sheila Peters, Rick Gatward, and Rachel Hood, and to those who helped me clarify my thoughts at crucial points – Frances Plummer, Diana Houlston and Jill Sharp – as well as Bonnie Tall, Maggie Jee, Philip Boys, Tilly Christie, Sarah Tall, Wendy Tall, and Helen Davison for unwavering support.

I'm grateful to my writing friends for encouragement, inspiring conversations and technical feedback – particularly Kathryn Lee, Felice Rhiannon, Cathie Wallace, Maggie Alexander, Jan Barton, Michael Brown and Rachel Wegh. Friends and colleagues at Hampshire Writers' Society, too, where there is always a patient ear, and helpful advice. I've done several Arvon residential courses and in one-to-one tutorials each of these excellent tutors has come up with an observation or piece of advice that has nudged me forward – John-Paul Flintoff, Alice Jolly, Bidisha, Will Self, Angela Clarke, Rory MacLean, and Amy Liptrot. Thank you. And a special mention for Anne Robin, not strictly speaking a writing friend but your enthusiasm and our wide-ranging conversations inspire me so much. I'd never have got started without you.

This is the third book cover that Jo Dalton has done for me and it's always a thrill to hand my creative output over, and to know that she will interpret it in a surprising and delightful way. Sincere appreciation to Dawn Black for the beautiful and charming interior design. Joanna Barnard, as editor, has helped me sharpen various themes, and Lindley Owen has been a generous and sharp-eyed beta-reader. Thank you for laughing in all the right places, asking smart questions, and calling me out on my aversion to commas. I am now a reformed punctuationist. And forever grateful.

This comes with much love to my grown-up children and their partners who are full of interesting ideas and challenge me to see the world through different eyes – and to Mike who continues to be the best treat of all.

While working as a research psychologist, Lynn Farley-Rose became fascinated by how people cope when things get tough. Her first book *31 Treats And A Marriage* is a personal account of reconnecting with life after unforeseen calamities, and in *The Interview Chain* she talks to remarkable people about things that help to make the world a kinder and more connected place. She grew up by the sea in Devon, and then lived in London until a move to rural Sussex resulted in a complete change of lifestyle. At one point she was responsible for the welfare of thirty-two animals and eight species including her four children. She now lives in Hampshire and loves her adult children but has no pets. You can read her blog at treatsandmore.com.

www.ingramcontent.com/pod-product-compliance
Lightning Source LLC
Chambersburg PA
CBHW020339010526
44119CB00048B/531